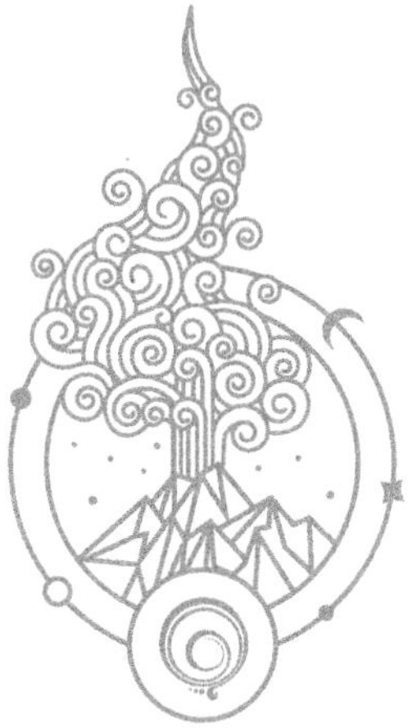

DEDICATED TO

the wise monks, and Bani Shorter
who taught me to survive and
thrive in difficult times.

AND TO

Michelle Dawn Silcox, my beloved,
for helping me to shine.

PRAISE FOR

HOW TO Survive & Thrive In Challenging Times

"I would like to say an enormous THANK YOU to Piers Cross.
His book saved my life and helped me survive a difficult time in my life.
His book gave me huge encouragement and support.
I was more calmed than before.
I believe that everything comes at the right time in life,
and this book came exactly when I needed it most.
Thank you, Piers."

— *Gabriela Galasinska, personal trainer and founder of FitnessGabi*

"This is the right book at the right time.
While the whole world is suffering from fear and uncertainty
because of the Coronavirus, this book is exactly what I needed.
It's like a lighthouse in rough seas, and you will find
most of your burning questions answered.
As it addresses each and every area of your life,
you will navigate through tough times and find yourself
renewed on the other side. This book will be like a faithful friend."

— *Christian Zikes, Men's High Performance Coach*

HOW TO Survive & Thrive In Challenging Times

101 Ways To Cultivate Resilience, Wellbeing & Inner Peace In All Areas Of Your Life

Piers Cross

HOW TO Survive
& **Thrive**
In Challenging Times

First published in Great Britain in 2008

www.Piers-Cross.com

ISBN: 979 8 6424 2103 1

Table Of Content

Table Of Content FOR EXERCISES

Table Of Content

FOR EXERCISES

Preface

TO THE 3rd EDITION

It is now April 2020 and the world is currently going through some real challenges. The Coronavirus (Covid-19) has made it's way around the globe and many people that I see and hear are struggling.

A few weeks ago I sent this book to a client and a friend asking what he thought of it. Did I need to do some more editing and was it readable. His reply was, "Wow, the world needs to read this now – if there has ever been a time the world needs a book like this. It is now!"

So yesterday I posted on Facebook about the book to see if anyone was interested in it. And to my surprise many people mentioned that they wanted to read it.

As you can see I had some resistance to it going out into the world. Yes, I had it for sale on my website for many years but few people bought it so it came down a few years ago.

Why did I have resistance?

The story that I share was very painful to experience and in the book I expose many of my flaws and my failings. I talk about the many mistakes and mess ups that I have made. I talk about trying to take my own life, prostitutes, breakdown, drugs, drink, and self-harming. It is not pretty.

The other reason for my resistance is that I started to write this book in 2008 and called it The Wellbeing Way. I was a fresh faced 32 year old who was still very raw from the first 30 years of challenges. I had also not really learned humility. So the resistance comes because I am a perfectionist and I feel that this book needs going over again.

But that is my resistance. As my friend said, the world needs this book now. It will never be perfect. So I offer this book with my journey and all the techniques and tools that I learned to support you at this time.

Yes, I dived deep into the depths of darkness but I returned with gold.

How did I go through these challenges and still come out the other side?

You are about to find out.

I will leave you with this image of the butterfly coming out of the chrysalis. The butterfly can struggle for a long time crawling out of the chrysalis. But this struggle which can take hours, pumps the wings with the fluids which enable this beautiful creature to fly.

Without the challenges this butterfly would never take flight.

And so it is with us at this time. The earth and humanity is going through huge challenges. And as I learned in my own life it is through these challenges that strength, and wisdom can be awakened.

And so it will be with mother earth and its inhabitants – through these challenges we will learn to fly.

Making the wish that may this book and these words remind you that you are ready to fly.

Love and blessings,

Piers Cross
West Yorkshire, April 2020

Introduction

Welcome to How To Survive & Thrive in Challenging Times. It is a great pleasure that you have decided to join me for this journey. I have felt so blessed over the years with having such amazing teachers, helping me through challenging times that I felt a natural calling to start to document all that I had been through and all that I had learned.

The book you hold in your hands is a guide. It is a guide that I was passed on orally, experientially and in written form over many years through teachers, guides and through personal experience. This book is a guide to becoming well. It is a guide to reawakening to all that you are. No matter where you are or who you are, no matter what you feel you have become or what you feel you have done, this book is for you.

For those of you who feel so stressed with modern living, for those of you who wish to find another way of being, a way of ease, relaxation and flow then this book will be of help.

Becoming well is a journey and yet we have to start somewhere. One of my favourite sayings is:

"The journey of a thousand miles starts with the first step."

And maybe for you this is the first step. Maybe you have been at the cause of life instead of at the effect. That is to say that instead of living the life that you want, you have been living the life of everybody else. You have been doing what everyone expects of you rather than doing what you really want to be doing in life.

And maybe for you this is the second step. You have already started on your journey of becoming well and have started a program of self-healing. Maybe you have seen the changes that you need to start implementing in order to regain the love, balance and harmony you have known in your life before. If this is you then this book will be a wonderful support as you gather strength and momentum in your recovery.

And maybe for you this is a journey you have been walking for some time. This road to well being. You have come a long way and can now turn and see how far you have travelled along this path. And it feels really good. For you, this book can also act as a support, and help to give you strength when the journey becomes a little more arduous or life becomes a little challenging again.

On my own personal journey I have been at each of those points on the road. My childhood had been a mixed bag. I grew up with an alcoholic father who spent most of the time away at sea in the Navy. Life at home fluctuated from being relaxed and loving when it was just my mother, my sister and I, to being a dark place when my father returned from sea.

At the age of 5 my father had cirrhosis of the liver and then spent a year in and out of hospital close to death. He survived, left the Navy and moved back home full time. It was a challenging time as a family and individually and I tried to run away from home many times. My father had a terrible temper and my parents would often argue. I too inherited my father's tempestuous nature and was also quick to anger – several times I fought physically with my father.

I eventually got my wish of leaving home and was allowed to go to boarding school at age 11. The first 3 weeks were wonderful – being away from my family – I had such fun. But then I realised that I wanted to go home and yet I couldn't – I had been told that boarding school was the safest place for me in case my father died. It suddenly dawned on my that I was stuck there. Emotionally I terrorized myself to not allow any emotion to show. I used the model of my aggressive, terrifying father to self-regulate myself. Any sign of tears or anger or any emotion really and I would internally ravage myself at how useless I was and how I was just being a little child. At boarding school emotion meant weakness – whether rage, tears or excitement and was jumped upon by my peers. And gradually my emotions disappeared into a deep dark pit.

I learned to tow the line after that and did what I was told (mainly – I started drinking at age 13) and I did everything I could to suppress all my emotions.

After many years of hoop jumping I arrived at one of the top business schools in Europe. From being a creative writer and painter as a child, I graduated school focusing on Maths, French and Business Studies – I had literally become a different person. Indeed, during the 7 years I was at boarding school I changed my name from Piers to Simon and called myself by the nickname Ziggy. I had created a sub-personality and had become someone else.

I spent 2 years at university in France and then while I was at university in London doing a work placement a little light opened in my armour. It was the late 90s and I had just had a difficult breakup with a long term partner and was feeling down. My way of dealing with challenges till that point had been to drink or take drugs or repress my emotions.

Instead I was shown a different option. Something magical. My sister lent me a self-help book by Susan Jeffers and I started to read it on the commute from North London down to Zone 5 in South London. I found it a revelation. There was another way, I found out, to dealing with this stuff inside of me. Rather than repressing, or depressing myself through too much drink, drugs and lack of self-care, I started to do something different.

Now at that time, I used to hang out with the drink and drug takers but I had never felt I fitted in. I didn't feel I had anything to say to them and I don't think they felt very easy around me either – essentially I was a psychopath with a hard impenetrable shell – a bit like my father really. And yet, here in this first book which was followed by many others over the years, I found ways to start to being with what I was feeling. Realising that maybe there wasn't anything wrong with me and that I didn't need to take lots of drugs, or drink myself into a stupor in order to deal with the uneasiness I felt inside myself.

There was another way. And yes, it took time and I admit that I fell over many times. Many times during my London years I wanted to give up and yet I kept going. Life became overwhelming at one point and I decided to move out of London and the City job I was doing. Within a few weeks my life had collapsed. From one minute to the next it all changed. I went from living in an exclusive area in London with my long-term partner, with a well-paid job for a Fortune 500 company to living on sofas and dirty beds, eventually quitting my job.

What happened? I realised I was living a lie of a life. I was with a partner who I didn't love, in fact, I realised that I had never loved anyone – I was an emotional wreck. I was doing a job I hated, living in a place where I felt dead. It was time to move. And yet to move was a huge upheaval – to leave my long-term partner for a second time in 5 years, leaving the security of my house and eventually leaving my City job. I felt depressed, suicidal and didn't know what to do. Somehow during this time I forgot about my practices.

During that time my father was diagnosed with terminal cancer and my already shaking foundations wobbled a little more. And yet in some ways it helped. It helped to be helping others. To help my father meant that I could stop thinking about how bad I was feeling inside. It seemed though, that my father really didn't want me helping out. It seemed to humiliate him having his son there. To be weak when he had always been so strong. A few days before he died, I confronted him about the hatred I always felt from him and his reply was that his whole life had been an act.

With less and less ties around me I searched for some meaning outside of myself. I was still running from the inner me. I took a job working as a Volunteer Coordinator in Africa. I threw myself into the work but still felt wobbly inside. I started to drink heavily and after about a year in Africa I returned to the UK.

I was now aware that I was a mess on all levels. I had worked so hard and taken very little care of myself for so long that mentally, physically and emotionally I was wrecked. I had voices running round my head and I thought that I was starting to go crazy. I spent a week around New Year drinking solidly and spent about £1,000 on drinking, drugs and going to clubs. After a week of not seeing any daylight and drinking too much I realised something had to change or I might not survive much longer.

I called a friend and went to visit. For the first time in a week I started to see sunlight and sleep without drink inside me. It felt wonderful. I started to look for a retreat space. I needed a break, somewhere I could work and yet I wouldn't have to pay to stay. I knew that I was a mess and a few weeks would not be enough. I had abused myself for 15 years and now I needed to do some healing.

I found a retreat space in Devon and went to visit for 3 weeks. While I was there

I met with one of the meditation teachers who recommend that I visit one of the Buddhist monasteries based in Hampshire. I contacted them but they said that were on Winter retreat and were not taking visitors. The teacher then recommended another Buddhist monastery in the north of England. He spoke with the abbot who said that I could come and help cook for 10 days in their Winter retreat. I agreed and set off up north with 2 bags.

On my journey north I was offered a job working for the same volunteer company in a position in Thailand. I would be the country manager, with car, full salary and I presumed a house. An amazing offer. I told them that I was on retreat and that I would let them know in 2 weeks time.

Now I won't go into details of my full monastic experience as I will talk more about stories from the monastery in the rest of the book. Just to say that I went for 10 days and ended up staying for 1000 days! Call it karma, good luck or bad luck everything unfolded perfectly.

After the first 2 weeks I realised more deeply that I was in the right place and that going to Thailand would be the worst possible thing for me. I was not in a fit state to be going anywhere!

I applied for and was given the job of the monastery's office manager and I took care of the accounts. After about 4 months of being in the monastery I realised that I might as well become a Novice monk seeing as I had committed to doing the office job for a year.

I had had many realizations up to this point but something shifted when I took robes and became a Novice monk. It was almost as if I now had permission to fall apart. Everything I had been running from for all these years, with all that drink, suppression and repression came rushing back to the surface.

Boy, oh boy was it difficult. Boy oh boy was it the most challenging time of my life. For about 2 years I went through the spinner, so to speak. I went through the washing cycle of life – literally every part of me was taken apart, spun 100 times a second and then left to drip dry. I cried most days for the best part of 2 years. I woke crying in my sleep most nights for a year, nightmare after nightmare resurfacing in my consciousness. I self-harmed, I tried suicide, I tried everything apart from the drink and the drugs. In fact all the things that I had used in the past to deny feeling and dealing with myself were not available – TV, internet, music, sexual contact with myself or with others, going out, drinking, drugs, eating after midday. All these things were off menu. I was literally going cold turkey on life.

I worked out at the time that the only things that were available to me were: reading, writing, sleeping (till 5am...), exercise, painting, meditation and working.

In essence I started to do battle with my inner tyrant – my alcoholic father I had used in boarding school. And that part of me was vicious. It had served to protect me for many years and had done an amazing job protecting the little child but now as an adult it was having devastating consequences. I was emotionally dead, drinking heavily and felt like I was going crazy. Now that I started to challenge this part of myself and not do everything it said, it would fly into a rage, and with the same aggression that this part of me had protected me, it now started to come at me physically until my own fists started beating me black and blue.

Now why on earth didn't you leave, I hear you saying. Don't worry I asked myself that question many times every day.

To be honest, I could not leave. Really I could not leave. I will repeat again, I could not leave. Oh, I wanted to, oh I so wanted to. But you see I stopped communication with my family, had very few friends and was in absolute turmoil – physically I had had a breakdown and could hardly get out of bed, emotionally I was self-harming and crying constantly, and mentally I had a thousand voices shouting at me, at how pathetic I was. So leaving wasn't an option.

And the other option was suicide. But I was learning from my Buddhist studies that to commit suicide meant that I would go into a hell realm for an indeterminable time.

I really felt like I was between a rock and a really hard place.

What on earth do you do?

It was around this time that I heard a story by Ajahn Chah who was the abbot's teacher. Ajahn Chah was the abbot of the monastery Wat Pah Pong in North East

Thailand and in the 60s and 70s had drawn to him a lot of Western disciples due to his relaxed, wise and loving way. The story went that Ajahn Chah had been having a strange meditation for a period of time. In the meditation he saw himself walking along a bridge until he could go no further. He then realised that he could not go back either. And the final realization was that he could no longer stand still.

Ajahn Chah puzzled with this image for quite a time before meeting another forest monk. He told the monk his story and asked him what he thought. The wise monk's reply was. "When you can't go forward, you can't go backward and you can't stand still this is where you practice..." Finally Ajahn Chah understood.

And finally I started to understand. For indeed I felt in that exact same position. I could not go forward – I couldn't leave the monastery; I could not go back – commit suicide; and I couldn't stand still – being with all that was assailing me in every moment was very challenging. So this was where I started to practice.

I started to wake up and in some moments of not being able to go forward, nor back, nor stand still I found peace. I found bliss. Just for a moment, I realised that there was something else out there. And so my healing journey really started. I had been living with some of the wisest beings I had ever met and slowly their teachings started to sink in. It took time and patience and the support of some amazing people. One of the supporters of the monastery was a contemporary of Jung and was an incredible Jungian Analyst. The intensity of how we worked was pretty amazing. I used to commute 6-7 hours once a week to see her and then spend 3-4 hours in session with her non stop. And something started to shift. I was learning some amazing things, tools and techniques for being well. I learned how to start to let go and find peace. The chink of light got bigger and bigger until I started to take care of Piers. I started to feel better within myself. I still had my challenges but felt so much stronger.

After about 3 and a half years I was meeting with the abbot and he asked me whether I wanted to commit for another year (we had done a rolling year to year commitment). I didn't know. He asked for an answer within a week. At the end of the week, half of me wanted to stay half of me wanted to go. I took a decision. I decided to leave.

Leaving was a challenge in itself. After all I had been through the monastery had become a safe container, a safe haven. To leave was to let that go, but I did feel strong enough.

As I settled back into everyday living, girlfriends, jobs, and eating after midday... I found that I was coping really well. In fact, a lot of the tools and techniques that I had learned in the monastery were meaning that I wasn't getting stressed. And when I did fall off the straight and narrow. I had the tools to pull myself through.

I decided to go back to work in the corporate environment again, mainly out of financial need. Although I had not had to pay for my time in the monastery I had spent all my savings on seeing therapists and other such things. I found it a challenge to start off with being back in that environment but through the tools that I had learned I started to cope. In fact, I started to do really well and most of my colleagues were really interested in my time in the monastery. And they wanted to learn.

I started up a meditation and well being class in my company. Within an hour of the message going out to my colleagues, the class was full. This was what so many people needed – so many people were stressed... And from there I started to teach others online and personally.

So this book is for you. This book is how I managed to turn it around. From being at the darkest of hours, as low as I could be to finding myself here. Still alive and happy. Sure, I still have my challenges and yet I seem to be able to cope better and better as the years go by.

This book is about you and about how you too can enter into this stream of well being. For if I can do it, I know that you can do it too. A lot of the tools in this book have been around for thousands of years and some I came up with myself. Some tools are easy to do and some will take a little practice. Some practice will take no effort and some will take determination. But all of these practices will take you in one direction: towards wellness, towards happiness and relief.

But it will take a little work. I personally recommend to the people I coach getting into a routine on a daily basis. This means doing the practices which I teach in this book for at least 30 minutes a day. What I say to people is set your alarm for 30 minutes before you usually get up and do some of the practices. Indeed this was one of my key healings and realizations in the monastery. We had a daily routine and no matter how I felt, even if I could hardly get out of bed, I still took part in this routine.

And by doing so I started to see that sometimes I felt okay and sometimes I felt awful and yet the world kept turning. What I came to realise is that I needed to let go of the okay times, the great times and the awful times. And by having a routine, a structure with which to unfold into I started to see the nature of reality. That everything is changing all the time and that I could relax and let go into that.

So throughout these pages you will find the tools, techniques and teachings that I received from the monks and the experiences. You will receive the insights I learned from the pitfalls and slip ups that I made.

Towards the end of each chapter you will find a little story from my own life; a mini autobiography. I share these to show that I have had some challenging times and some amazing times, and yet I have come out the other side. These contrasting life experiences have been so important to my self-development. Without them I would not be here sharing what I now know. So whatever challenges you are faced with, have courage, see that the strength is within you to overcome them and then integrate these experiences into your own life. You are an amazing being. In these pages you will start to unfold into your amazingness

One last thing to leave you with before you too embark on this amazing journey is to tell you about the monks. The monks showed such kindness, love, generosity, compassion, patience and gentleness towards me. Without them I would not have got through it. Without the monks' guidance and teachings I would be in a very different place than I am today.

They were there for me in a time of great change and eventually great transformation. And in the same way the monks were there for me, so this book and this wisdom is here for you too. You are worth so much, you are such an amazing, brilliant being and I thank you again for being here.

Another important point is that yes, this is a continual journey. I am still learning; I am still a student and I always will be a student as I enjoy learning so much. To think that I never go through challenges or to think that by reading this book will mean you never go through challenges is erroneous. The most challenging times are our greatest teachers. They are our greatest gift. So by sharing my own stories I show you that through my darkest times I have found light and healing. And therefore through your darkest times, you too can find light, healing and happiness.

How To Use This Book

You can either read this book cover to cover or go to the section that you feel relates to you the most at this time: that might be relationships or work, health or holidays.

What I would recommend is that you read it through completely once and then when things come up in life around the different areas then you go straight to that section and follow the advice and exercises on offer.

By reading through once you will see that many of the tools and techniques available could be applied to any area of your life. Having the full picture then allows you to see that in this book there are many different ways of becoming well.

A key theme which runs throughout this book is one of the most valuable lessons that I have learned. That of being gentle, being kind to yourself, allowing yourself to heal and become well in a holistic and healthy way.

What to do if in need of quick pick me up?

The best place to start if you need a quick stress relief fix is to go here: Exercise 19: Counting To 10 (P. 168) & Exercise 21: Communicating From A Calm & Assertive Place (P. 187).

Please make notes on this book, bend it, fold it, make it second nature to you. Come back to it when something in your life stresses you and you need instant relief. Don't be stubborn, use the resources that you have and I am one of them!

What I would also recommend is that you find yourself a journal or notebook of some kind. Most post offices or stationery stores will have them or you could pick one up rather cheaply on Amazon or Ebay. There are quite a few exercises in here which will require you to do some writing. So buy yourself a new notepad or use one you have lying around the house or office. It's important that you don't show the journal to others at the beginning, in recovering a sense of well-being we need to start trusting ourselves. And one of the ways is allowing ourselves the space to express what we are feeling. By not showing the journal to others allows us to start trusting in the process.

Some of the tips and techniques will work wonderfully for you and some won't. That's okay, that's completely normal.
Some of the techniques will work for a while and then stop suddenly. That's normal as well. The mind catches up with what you are doing and tries to limit you. Try something new.

The things which didn't work will suddenly start working. And vice versa. And then the things which did work but then didn't suddenly start to work again. Strange how the mind works but what I would suggest is persevere. Keep practising the tools and very quickly you will feel wellness filling you.

I personally found that things which worked really well for me suddenly would stop working. I would find a wonderful technique only for it to stop working after a week or so.

In the end I had learned so many tools and techniques that I had a whole array of amazing techniques. I liken this to a toolbox. Well, this toolbox you will find inside.

I am so happy you are here, so joyful that you are choosing the way into well-being. Thank you for allowing me to share.

Piers Cross
West Yorkshire, UK

CHAPTER 1

Using Exercise To Rejuvenate Your Mind, Body & Spirit

There are many pathways to managing stress and moving towards well-being. Within these pages I am sharing what I have found and what I have been taught over the past 15 years to work in creating a sense of well-being. One of the most powerful tools I have learned and still use to this day is that of exercise.

Exercise has been a life saver for me. Now exercise for me is a broad subject and over this chapter I will go into some depth about what exercises have indeed been a life saver for me and have worked with my clients. From yoga to walking, from swimming to tai chi we will look at and discuss the different forms of exercise that are considered the most powerful for relieving stress.

And yet within this it is important to note that these are my own personal findings or the teachings of my teachers. What worked for them or work for me might be different from what works for you. It is important on this journey of self-discovery to find out what works best for you. What inspires you and motivates you in terms of exercise?

From a young age I was drawn to being outside. I loved being in the woods or swimming in the sea. It was such a pleasure to me to be running around and being physical. And when the challenges arose in my life as a child I chose to be outside. I would go for a walk, I would get outside, I would hide in the woods and no matter how bad I was feeling, by the time I came back I felt so much better.

It was like a program for me. Feel bad – get outside. No thought, no hesitation – outside now. And if truth be told this has saved my life on many occasions.

The power of exercise, the power of getting into the woods, getting outside cannot be underestimated. We as a race have become attached to being indoors, to being sedentary. And there is a time and place for this. A time for rest and respite is paramount but to do it to the degree where we hardly walk at all or spend any time doing exercise is no longer balanced.

What I am suggesting is that we as humans start to find balance again. To find a way of nurturing ourselves again. And one of the first places I personally always start with and when working with clients is with exercise.

As a society we are stressed. We have filled our time up. Over the course of this book I am proposing that we let go of certain elements that we have filled our time up with and replace with things which truly feed us.

Exercise is so powerful. And yet as a society we discount it as unimportant. Sure, we can spend the afternoon getting excited about sport but usually it is from the comfort of our own home. We have become voyeurs of the sporting act. It is time for us to connect again with our bodies. By doing so we become more present. We become happier. We become healthier.

And we start in a small way, this is what is being proposed. A lot of what I propose in this book will be baby steps not some giant leap. When we take giant leaps we often end up on our faces vowing never to be so stupid again. And yet when we take small, gentle steps, just like the parable of the tortoise and the hare, we end up moving mountains. A 5 minute walk once a day becomes 10 minutes, becomes 20 minutes, becomes an hour. By being gentle like the tortoise we can go an awfully long way.

One of the key teachings that I picked up from the Abbot I lived with was that we need to see ourselves like a small child. He used this analogy for meditation practice but it equally fits here. He said that if you were to imagine a small child learning to walk who kept falling over how would you react? Would you shout at the little child to work harder, to stop falling over or would you gently pick the child up and set them back on their feet again? Well of course, you reply, I would pick the child up. And when they fall over again you again pick them up again. And again... And you keep doing it for you know that eventually they will learn to walk.

And so it is with you. In this case with exercise, you take things gently, you take baby steps and when you fall over, you stop going to the gym, you stop walking, you stop running, you quit cycling, you pick yourself up again. No big deal. And every time you fall over you pick yourself up. Again and again and again.

So the following are some different pointers to help you gain some clarity into exercise, to help inspire you and to help you find the perfect exercise for you.

1. Find An Exercise You Love

This is quite an obvious point but you would be surprised how many people overlook this. Many people choose exercises to do that are either in fashion, are what all their friends are doing or what all their colleagues are doing. As I mention later on, having someone to do exercise with is really supportive, but it is also really important to start with something you love.

I work as a volunteer with Scouts working with the older end. One of my roles is to help guide the students with their Duke of Edinburgh award which is set of tasks and exercises they complete along with an expedition. What I have found over the years is that the boys and girls who choose something because it is easy or because their friends are doing it rarely even get started. The motivation isn't there. One of their tasks is to do a physical exercise for a period of 3, 6 or more months depending on the award they are doing. And the first question that I ask them are:

- What exercise are you passionate about?
- What physically do you really love to do?

And by doing this they tap into what they are passionate about. And most of the Scouts who are motivated by this follow through (not all though...) So reflect on this now – write it in your journal if you find this easier. In terms of exercise what is it that you love doing? What is it that you have always dreamed of doing? Maybe you were not allowed to do it as a child. Now is your chance.

Allow yourself to dream. And again remembering those baby steps. The first step is finding out if there is a class in what you love nearby. First step, simple. And if not, could you ask a teacher to come and teach in your town. And if that doesn't come off then what else could you do?

Becoming well is not a chore. It is joy, it is excitement, it is the re-birthing of yourself as alive, happy and vibrant. This process is fun, eye opening and playful. Let it be that way. What do you love in terms of exercise?

Whatever it is do that. Why?

Well, like I say, when you are passionate about something it is that much easier to get motivated about it. Some days you won't really feel up to exercising but if you have something you are really passionate about then you will go anyway. And from doing something regularly you then start to get into a routine – you are now exercising 5 times a week – it becomes normal and it feels great. So the place to start is with something you are passionate about.

Don't know, you say? Well, try something out that you like as a spectator sport. You probably know more about it than you would think. If you love watching rugby then go to a rugby training and see what you think, try it out. If you love watching Wimbledon or the US Open find a tennis club and give it a go. By trying things out you find out whether you like it or not. The key here obviously is trying it. Do it. Exercise is the first step to your amazing recovery.
Be aware of doing things you are not too keen on. You just don't have the same motivation. For example, everyone else is going to the gym so you feel you should go to the gym too. But you find it really boring and have to drag yourself there each week. After a few weeks you have stopped going.

But if you find something that really ticks all your boxes – exciting, fun, a laugh and makes you feel great, well, it's not so hard to keep yourself motivated.

Where I see the stumbling block for most people is the starting. Once you have started and got into a rhythm it's easy. Making the initial call or enquiry is the stumbling block. "Oh, I'll do it tomorrow. That can wait." Maybe it can wait but where possible do the work today to find and research the things you love. Pick up your journal and start jotting down ideas. And when you have 10 minutes look online today and make the calls you need to make to start your amazing new exercise.

Remember that it is baby steps. If it seems like a giant leap being fit and exercising regularly, start small. Look online, speak to a friend, write for 5 minutes in your journal – what do I love in terms of exercise? You can do it and you are doing it, well done!

2. Try Exercising With Others

Having coached different people over the years I have learned that a lot of individuals find doing exercise with others more motivating. For a lot of people doing exercise as a pair or a group is a good way to keep motivated. You get to benefit from others' drive and energy which pulls you along when you are not feeling motivated.

The key is firstly, do something that you love doing and secondly, if you are drawn to it and like the support then join a group or do it with friends. There is a downside to this, and it is that if your exercising partner stops, or the group stops then it is possible you stop as well.

This is why it is key to firstly do something you love. Therefore if your friend stops and bails, you still have the motivation to find someone else or find a group.

So try to balance this out. Do some exercise on your own which requires your own self motivation and find an exercise partner where you go off running or swimming, or some other exercise together.

There are many groups out there like running groups, walking groups, football, tennis, or swimming so you become part of a team. The team around you helps to keep you motivated and therefore when you don't really feel like exercising the group helps to lift you. It is your routine and you keep going.

3. Walking Is A Simple Yet Effective Stress Relief

Walking is key to managing stress. It is one of the most powerful exercises I have come across over the years. The sense of well-being, the sense of calm and how it helps to clear the mind, body and emotions is very powerful.

And yet in this modern world few of us walk much. We get in our cars, we take the bus or the taxi rather than walking. We take the lift or the escalator because it is easier and it is quicker. We seem to be forever living in the past or the future, worrying about what we are going to be doing later, about what time we are going to be getting to work so we try to do everything as quick as we can – we take the shortest, the quickest, the easiest route wherever we go rather than thinking about our health and our stress levels. If walking to work means we have to get up 30 minutes earlier it will rarely enter our consciousness. We don't see it as an option.

What I am suggesting is that by taking the time to walk on a regular, or even daily basis, and walking mindfully, aware of how you are feeling will transform your day and your stress levels.

When I worked as a nanny I used the take the younger kids to school every day. The routine that was in place when I arrived was that the mum would take the younger kids by car as she would would drop the older one off as well at another school. Time wise it was the most logical thing to do.

But as I didn't drive the only way for me to take the younger kids was by walking. They still wanted to go by car, obviously, it was much easier, more comfortable and they didn't have to walk. In fact, the younger kids really didn't like walking. So when I suggested that I take the younger kids on foot, the mum thought it was a great idea but the kids hated it.

And for a week or so they moaned and groaned and dug their heels in. But then they started to love walking. At the weekends we would walk to the local lake and walk around it finding magical spots and trees to climb. And they loved it.

Sure it was a struggle for a week or so but after that I got to walk and they got to walk. They got to clear their heads and I got to clear mine. It helped to balance them before school and got them fitter and healthier. And likewise for me.

Where in your life can you start to walk rather than taking the car, or bus, or train? Have you thought about getting off a stop early and walking the rest of the way. Maybe you catch a train and then a bus. Maybe the bus ride is 5 minutes – can you walk instead?

What about taking the stairs instead of the lift? It is surprising how often if we are at work we go up and down the building. By taking the stairs instead of a lift or escalator gets the heart going just a little bit, gets the muscles pumping just a little bit. But as I say over and over again baby steps. Start small and even if you don't manage that then that is fine as well. Really, I hear you say. Yes, remember it is all about being gentle and kind and we do what we can do. By being tough on ourselves gets the job done for a week, but we end up beating ourselves up when we don't manage the stairs, or when we take the car rather than walking. And that's okay really. Do what you can do – you are amazing.

If you can walk rather than take the train or bus then do it. Walking helps to clear the mind, exercise the body and bring grounding into your being – you feel more here.

Walking can be done anytime, anyplace, anywhere. You can be in a city or in the middle of the mountains and still you can walk. Indeed when I have been working in the middle of the city I regularly got out for a walk. I figured that the smokers went out every 2 hours so why couldn't I? I checked with my manager and she said of course. So I would go out twice a day for a 10 minute walk and a breath of fresh air. I will teach you the exercise I used to do for balancing out my mind on these breaks.

EXERCISE 1

Walking To Slow The Mind Down

READ THROUGH THE EXERCISE ONCE BEFORE TRYING IT OUT.

1. Give yourself 10 minutes for this exercise and make sure that you are not going anywhere or if you are there is no time limit to getting there. You will be walking slowly and it is important that you walk as slowly as you can.

2. Start walking at a normal pace. (you can practise this now wherever you are.)

3. If your mind is feeling very busy then walk fast. Match the thoughts you have in your head with the speed of your walk. For example, you have been in loads of meetings with lots of information and your head is spinning – so walk quickly.

4. Gradually start to slow your walking down. And as you do that start to breath deeply and more slowly

5. As your walking slows, start to press down with your big toes on the earth. That's right. Press down firmly and focus your attention in your big toes as you walk.

6. See how by pressing down on your big toes you start to walk more slowly. Soften and deepen your breath. Keep your attention on your big toes.

7. Gradually your mind will start to still. Be aware around of what is around you but keep your attention focussed on your toes. Continue practising this for around 10 minutes.

In my own life, walking has been key for my own sanity. As soon as I felt myself about to explode emotionally in the monastery, I got my walking boots on and I stepped outside.

It is strange that, the fact that when I feel challenged I just walk outside. But the truth is that it has saved me time and time again. Going for a walk when I have felt terrible rather than shouting my mouth off, or doing something I would regret for a long time has been a Godsend. By getting into this routine of doing an exercise like walking when we are feeling good means that when we don't feel so good we have trained ourselves so well that the natural thing is to continue on this positive, life-affirming act, even if we feel crap.

So for me, in the monastery, stuff would come up and I would literally head for the hills. Every day I would head for the hills or the woods. Every day. Well, there wasn't much I could do so walking became an extremely important part of my recovery.

I headed for the hills and walked. Some days I walked solidly for 5 or 6 hours even in the driving snow.

Did it make a difference? All I have to say in answer to that is, I am still here. I am still writing this now. So wherever possible, walk. If you take the kids to school, walk with them. If you have to go to town, walk if possible.

By taking a daily walk, you keep the body in shape and you start to feel wellness spreading through you. It is a powerful thing and it is one that I still do to this day.

You are the key to your own well-being so find some time today to go for a walk. Be it 5 minutes, 10 minutes or 2 minutes. And then do it again. You are so worth it.

4. Yoga

Yoga is an exercise which has been around for thousands of years; the earliest record of yoga is from around 3,000 BC in India. In the West we see yoga as a physical exercise but this is just one aspect of yoga – there are many other strands to the form of yoga practised in India.

Hindu monks first brought the teachings of yoga to the West at the end of the 19th century and the beginning of the 20th century. It was not until the 1980s that yoga really took off when research was done to show that yoga was really beneficial to heart health.

As of today yoga has gained a huge popularity across the world. In the USA alone there are now a proposed 20 million who practise some form of yoga.

My own journey with yoga started at the age of 14. I had been having back problems so I borrowed a yoga book and cassette from a family member and started to practise. I didn't find it very easy to practise on my own and wasn't up for doing any classes so didn't do it very regularly.

But once I arrived in the monastery and I met some of the supporters who were yoga teachers I started to get back into. I had been in the monastery 6 months or so when one of our supporters was visiting. It was possible to come and stay at certain times of the year and we would usually have a constant flux of visitors flowing through our walls.

One such visitor was a well known yoga teacher and he offered to teach some of the monastic residents yoga. Being a very physical person I jumped at the chance to learn some yoga from him. At one point he came to stay for about a month and in that time I learned a terrific amount of yoga.

The yoga he taught was called Astanga Yoga. It is a more physical form of the discipline, but I really enjoyed this type of exercise as I was not doing much else physically at the time apart from walking. I got really into practising the yoga and did it once a day. The yoga teacher visited again about 6 months later and he was amazed at how quickly I had picked it up – having not much else to focus my mind on meant that I did it regularly.

I recommend yoga as a stress relief and a way becoming well to one and all because there are so many different forms of yoga to suit every individual need. From yoga which is really gentle for the older person to the really physical yoga, all categories of people are catered for. One of my mother's friends who is in her 90s puts her daily practice of yoga down to her clear mind and good physical health. It shows that anyone can do it.

Some of the different forms of yoga are as follows:

- Hatha (gentle)
- Scaravelli yoga (a newer form which involves gentle movement)
- Astanga (more physical yoga – a really good workout)
- Kundalini yoga (very aerobic – great for clearing the mind)
- And many more

Having so many different forms of yoga means that there are yoga forms to fit everyone's needs. What I personally recommend is that you go to a class and try a few different forms out.

If you are more physical then maybe Astanga is for you or if you are looking for a more gentle exercise then maybe Hatha yoga is more your type.

Yoga combines movement and stretching with breathing. This means that at the end of a yoga session your breathing is deep and you have received a physical, emotional and mental workout (see how relaxed you feel).

The following exercise is the founding exercise in yoga called the sun salutation. As the name suggests it is a good exercise to practice every morning as the sun rises. It helps to stretch most of the body's muscle groups and is an excellent way to start the day.

EXERCISE 2

The Sun Salutation

PLEASE READ THROUGH THIS EXERCISE FIRST BEFORE PRACTISING THIS EXERCISE. PLEASE CONSULT YOUR DOCTOR OR PHYSICIAN BEFORE DOING ANY FORM OF PHYSICAL EXERCISE.

1. Please find enough space so that you can easily stretch out horizontally for the whole length of your body in a heated or warm room. You will need to be wearing loose fitting clothing for this exercise.

2. Stand with your feet together on a yoga mat or a carpet so that there is space for the length of your body to stretch out behind you.

3. Take a deep breath in and centre your attention on your belly.

4. As you breathe out relax your shoulders.

5. As you breathe in again stretch both arms upwards so that they meet above your head, both palms touching.

6. As you **breathe out** bend forward from the hips bringing your hands to touch the floor (you may also grab your legs, ankles or wherever you can reach while keeping your legs straight).

7. As you **breathe in** while keeping your hands in the same position look up with your head and straighten your back. You should feel a stretch on the backs of your legs.

8. As you **breathe out** leaving your hands in the same position, step back into a press-up position so that your arms, back and legs are straight. As you continue breathing out bend the arms and lower the body.

9. As you **breathe in** you roll on your toes forward and arch your body backwards so that your head and back are arched upwards.

10. As you **breathe out** you roll back on your toes so that your body is now in a V shape where your body and legs join. Upper body, legs and arms are straight. Widen your feet so that they are shoulder width apart. This is called a downwards dog in yoga. Hold this position for **5 in and out breaths**.

11. As you **breathe in** bring your legs forward to your hands so that you are holding the same position as in 7. Feet and legs together.

12. As you **breathe out** you bend your head down towards your legs so that you are back in position 6.

13. As you **breathe in** straighten your body and stretch up with your hands so that they are touching palm to palm as in position 5.

14. As you **breathe out** bring your hands to your sides.

15. Repeat up to 5 times.

5. Tai Chi and Qigong

Tai Chi and Qigong are ancient Chinese forms of exercise and relaxation. Millions of Chinese practise these forms on a daily basis – if you have ever visited China you will testify to the thousands of people lined up in the parks every morning.

Tai Chi and Qigong work on a similar basis to yoga in that they work at re-energising the body through movement. In yoga, energy is called Prana and in Chinese it is called Chi or Qi.

By practising different forms of movement while focusing on the breath you stimulate the chi. The result is that the mind settles, the body feels invigorated and you feel relaxed yet centred.

I have personally been practising and teaching Qigong for 13 years and am constantly amazed at how good this practise makes me feel. Indeed, I feel centred and balanced and whatever fears or anxieties I have had before evaporate quickly.

The students that I have taught over the years have sometimes struggled with meditation as their minds were too busy. So to start off with I get them doing a few qigong exercises to still the mind. Then when I reintroduce meditation they find it much easier to relax and let go of their thoughts.

EXERCISE 3

Qigong - Lifting Arms Through Water

PLEASE READ THROUGH THIS EXERCISE FIRST BEFORE PRACTISING

1. It is best to be done in loose fitting, comfortable clothing but any clothing is fine as well.

2. Stand with your legs shoulder width apart with your feet parallel facing forward. Bend your knees slightly and rotate your hips so your back is straight.

3. Relax your shoulders and breathe deeply.

4. Place your hands parallel to the ground, fingers facing forward in front of the hips and at waist height. There should be a 3-6 inch gap in between the hands and the body at all times.

5. Take another deep breath in and out and relax the shoulders. Become aware of how you are feeling.

6. As you breathe in again slowly bring your hands upwards. As the breath reaches its zenith when the hands are about shoulder height start to breathe out. Bring the hands back to waist height, making sure the body is relaxed.

7. Repeat step 6 for a total of 9 times and then rest.

8. You can also imagine your hands are moving through water and that you can feel a certain resistance pushing against your hands.

9. Before going on to do something else, be still. Allow yourself to become aware of how you feel now after doing the exercise.

Excellent... Qigong is a really powerful grounding exercise and helps to still the mind. Try the exercise out and see how you feel. Start to allow the exercises in this book to become body knowing. That is to say that you start to become aware of how the body feels before and after the exercises. Do you feel calm, relaxed, at ease, happy, peaceful? Or maybe not. Note the responses – allow them to become body knowing.

The body will tell you what it needs. If it feels good then it really likes it, if not it doesn't or maybe your need to read through the exercise again and see that you are doing it correctly.

If you are drawn to one of the exercises in the book then I would recommend that you find a teacher so that you can learn more fully about the practices and the nuances of each discipline.

6. Other Forms of Exercise For Managing Stress

Other forms of exercise that I have tried and recommend (please check with a medical doctor before starting any new health regime) are:

- Running / jogging
- Working out in a gym
- Martial arts
- Dancing

Running / jogging: Running is a very powerful way of getting fit and getting outside. If you live near the countryside or the seaside it can be a wonderful way of exercising outdoors. Running can be very grounding and can help to release a lot of tension from both the mind, emotions and the body.

It is not for everyone but if you have done this before or even if not, but are drawn to this then it is a great way of returning to wellness.

Start off slowly and gradually build up the distances that you run. Where possible try running in nature as your body benefits from the fresh air filling your lungs.

There are running clubs that you can join or you can ask a friend to join you. Once you get into a rhythm you will find that you really enjoy your daily or weekly run.

Working out in a gym: Gyms are pretty amazing places nowadays. Very different from even 10 years ago. Hi-tech machines, music videos, every type of class that you would want to do and more.

A gym is certainly a place to go if you need motivation or stimulation to do any exercise.

I personally love going to gyms nowadays because I find the swimming, the range of machines you can use and the facilities to be great. But I was not always this enthused and I used to find myself rather bored, they didn't have the music and the videos when I was a teenager. Nowadays, I find the music and the videos can be a bit overpowering but I know for others this can add the motivation to run the extra mile on the treadmill or to cycle the extra 5 minutes on the bike.

Going to gym after work can be a powerful way of releasing the tensions from your day and boosting your energy levels. Many gyms have free trials so I would recommend you have a go and see if it is for you.

Martial arts: Martial arts are a really good way of channelling any worries or stress into a really positive and cathartic release. By being really physical you allow yourself to get in touch with your body. And by practising martial arts you help to release stress and get fit at the same time.

Many martial arts work with the breath so this can help to stabilise the mind and the emotions. The discipline involved in martial arts can spread to other areas of your life. Maybe you need the discipline to say no to others or maybe it is learning to say no to yourself when you are trying to take too much on. Martial arts can help to form those healthy habits.

I personally have been doing martial arts now since I was a teenager when I started to learn karate and judo. I have trained with Chinese Shaolin Kungfu disciples and spent several years practising different martial arts.

I find that martial arts are really good for channelling any aggression and anger which arises from stress. This energy can be channelled into a very positive and cathartic release, and as a way of getting very fit.

I found that I would go through phases of practising martial arts in the monastery daily. Personally this allowed me to release the tension that I had been holding onto for so many years. It took time and a lot of patience, but it felt really good to be physical and to channel the energy I was feeling. I was able release the emotions which were coming up in a really positive way – getting fit.

It is important to remember when starting to get in touch with inner emotions that there can be a huge backlog of unfelt emotions inside. I feel that we can have a dam inside of ourselves which we have blocked up – no emotion, feeling or unpleasant sensation is released from us.

When you start to get in touch with this inner emotion it can feel overwhelming. But be patient. Going to a martial arts class and having a teacher hold a safe space can allow this channelling of energy flow in a positive way.

It might well take time – it took me 2 or 3 years of feeling and dealing with my unfelt emotions and stress before I felt that I had released the water from the dam, the anger from within.

So martial arts and exercise are a wonderful way of getting in touch with inner emotions because otherwise we store this unfelt emotion in our bodies. And yes, if we don't release it, it can become sickness.

By working out and connecting to yourself you start to release the stress that you have been storing up inside like this inner dam. Through this work you can gradually start to release it.

Dancing: Dancing is a powerful release. And nowadays, like at the gym, there are so many classes and teachers to choose from. Maybe you have watched an amazing film or TV show about dancing and thought, "Wow, that's cool, I would love to try that!" Well, now's your chance.

Whether it was watching Strictly Ballroom, or Street Dance, or Honey, or one of the other amazing films about dancing have a go. Dancing can be so freeing. It can again help to release tension; free the mind from the thoughts of the day so you feel clear and at ease.

Dancing can also be an amazing way of reconnecting with your partner, or it can a great way of meeting an amazing partner. Salsa, tango, rumba, ballroom dancing... they all require a partner and this can help to build trust and connection in a partnership. For some of the styles of dancing you have to almost work intuitively with your partner. And this, in itself, helps you to develop intuition in your relationship – you know when to have time apart, or when you partner could do with a hug. A powerful thing dancing.

Another powerful aspect of dancing as a couple is the fact that you must really embody the male or female perspective. This is to say that if you are the male in a partnership then you must learn how to lead, to know where you are going, to be present (to not tread on your partner's feet). If you are female then you learn to let go and be led by the male. For both parties this can be very challenging. Many men feel emasculated and the thought of leading can be very daunting. And for some women, the idea of being led by someone else can bring up real rage - "I'm an independent woman and I can take care of myself!" Learning to let go for both parties can be a powerful healer.

And then there are the dances and classes which you do mostly on your own. Gabrielle Roth's Five Rhythms is a great form of dance and exercise. Most classes last for a couple of hours and the class moves through 5 rhythms – flowing, staccato, chaos, lyrical and stillness. So you dance slowly – warming up, then a bit more powerfully with staccato, then you really let go with chaos, relaxing into lyrical and then letting go completely with stillness. It is a very powerful dance and is a drink and drug free space.

To dance without alcohol is a powerful thing. Most of us are conditioned to dance only after having drunk a certain number of drinks or taken the prerequisite number of drugs – this was certainly the case for me.

But to dance without alcohol is so freeing. For a start you don't fall over and you have an amazing sense of balance. Also, you have rhythm which flows over you once you have relaxed at the strangeness of not being drunk.

The first time I tried to dance without drinking so much fear came up for me. I wanted to attend a 5 Rhythms' class. While I was walking to the class the internal dialogue of, "You shouldn't be doing this, you're a fool, you can't dance, what are you doing!" was going crazy in my head. I felt such fear but...I had an amazing time. It felt so good to move the body consciously rather than unconsciously (how I used to when I was drinking). I was always into Nirvana – a grunge rock band – as a teenager so when we got to chaos and the dance teacher put on some Nirvana I felt right at home!

So find a local dance class – I would really recommend Five Rhythms but if there is not one locally go to salsa or tango – or something you've always wanted to do but never had the courage. Have the courage now because not only your body but your emotions would love you to dance now!

7. Swimming

Swimming is one of the most valuable forms of exercise. The physical exertion combined with being in water in a powerful combination. Water is cleansing for the physical and yet it is also cleansing for the emotions and for the mind.

Whether it is that we are made up of 70% water that makes being in water so healing, it is not clear. What is clear is how we feel after we have been in water – be it a bath, a swimming pool, the ocean or a river. We feel invigorated, refreshed, clear headed, present... Indeed, exercising in water is extremely healing.

In my own life I put the healing powers of water down to being able to deal with stress and anxiety while working in a busy office.

I had been out of the monastery for about a year when my funds ran out. I had no money and started to claim unemployment benefit. After a period of time I found work back in the same environment I had left when I quit London many years before. It was a strange return to be working for a big American corporation again as I had vowed never to return to the corporate world when I had left London.

And at the beginning it felt like my idea of a nightmare...

The first day I walked into my new office....

It was open plan so there were around 90 desks sprawled over this huge space. One of my colleagues likened it to a spaceship with round air conditioning vents rising up from the ground to the ceiling.

And for the first day I was sat in front of a computer reading training manuals for a system I knew nothing about.

This is when the headaches started…

And within a week I started to feel truly awful: headaches, feeling sick and really low on energy. But I had just started the job so didn't feel I could take any time off.

That first weekend after the job had started I woke up on Saturday morning vomiting with serious headaches. I could hardly move my body and I felt awful.

I caught a taxi to Accident and Emergency in the local hospital. They couldn't see anything wrong with me so sent me home. I spent the next few days in bed feeling really sick without a clue what was wrong. I returned to work feeling a little better but still struggled to be in this big office.

It was summertime in Brighton, which is an English city on the south coast, so I decided to make two changes which completely healed my sickness.
The first was to buy a little gadget called a Q-Link which helps against the EMF (Electromagnetic fields) radiation of computers.

And the second?

I started to swim 3 or 4 times a week in the sea. It was amazing and I see that this was the thing that healed me the most.

I would leave work at 5pm and head straight to the beach. I would then swim for half an hour to an hour. And the change was tremendous.

Whatever stress or worry I had got washed away. I remember that most days I would leave the office with a fog around my head – this manifested itself as not being able to think clearly or as headaches. And yet amazingly after half an hour in the sea it had completely cleared. I felt great. I could think again.

EXERCISE 4

Swimming

1. Do some research online and find the nearest swimming pool or safe place to swim. If you live in a warm climate and it is possible to swim in the sea, or lake, or river then do some research around this and find the perfect spot for you.

2. Take it easy to start off with. If you have not been swimming or done exercise for a while start off slow. Before going into the water really centre yourself by breathing deeply 3 times in the centre of your belly. Feel how you feel.

3. Make a goal. Maybe it is to swim 50 metres outside, along a river for 100 metres, or do 10 lengths without stopping. And stick by it.

4. Repeat the affirmations: "I am strong and fit." "I am letting go of my thoughts," "I am bringing healing to myself."

5. Feel the invigoration of being in the water and when you have finished what you set yourself check in again – how do you feel?

6. Repeat as often as possible.

Swimming is powerful, there is no doubt. Take the time to do the above exercise and watch how your stress levels drop away just as they did mine. You have a powerful ally in swimming so make good use of it.

8. Exercising In Nature

Any form of exercise is good for stress relief as you are engaging your body rather than just your mind. As has been stated before exercise clears the mind and helps emotions and stresses to settle.

But an even better way of gaining benefits from exercise is to do it outside. And especially in nature: the countryside, in a park, by the sea or a lake. This is how you gain extra benefit from exercise.

Not only do you gain from a cardiovascular workout but you also gain from the fresh air and the fact of being outside.

It is difficult to explain in words but if you are to reflect back on how you feel after a walk in nature, you will understand what I am saying.

There is something very healing about being in nature. No matter how you felt before you walked outside the door, by the time you have entered the woods or reached the top of a mountain, you feel totally different. Nature holds us and de-stresses us. That is its gift to us.

Research from Japan and especially, Shinrin-yoku – Forest Bathing, shows that there are many health benefits from being outside and particularly under trees. Trees release a chemical called phytoncides which defends against disease and insects. This chemical has been shown to reduce physiological stress and lower blood pressure and heart rates in humans(Qing Li).
So where possible make an effort to get outside while exercising; to breathe in the fresh air and touch nature so that it touches you back and rejuvenates you.

Drink in its beauty and allow it to wash away your fears and stress.

Exercise was something I always took for granted. From a young age I had always been a talented sportsman. My father and grandfather had both represented their counties in athletics and hockey respectively and I also had this same natural athleticism.

My communication wasn't great as a teenager while at boarding school for obvious reasons – the inner tyrant meant that people kept away from me and I hardly spoke during the day as a form of self-defence. I found that the easiest thing was to keep myself to myself and not say anything. This didn't really translate to a sports field especially where you have to shout a lot if you want to receive the ball!

But I loved sports and exercise was a form of release for me – a channel for my anger at being in a place I didn't want to be. And a boarding school was a great place to be doing sports – there were team games every day plus we did PE regularly.

Exercise was one of the ways I escaped. Exercise was one of the ways that I learned to channel my rage and aggression in a "positive" way. I loved playing rugby and used my internal anger to make myself into a powerful player.

At the age of 13 this all changed. I injured my back playing cricket and had to stop playing sport for a year. It devastated me. From having a channel for my unhappiness suddenly I had no release. I didn't know what to do so I went inwards – I started to read lots and read lots of horror. I started to get into quite a dark space.

I started to become very depressed and started to contemplate suicide. I couldn't stay in this school and yet I couldn't leave without my parents' permission. Suicide was the only way out. (I did hear of another way out years later – getting expelled. But I was too frightened of my father's wrath to try that one!)

One day I visited the school doctor and told him how I was feeling; that I wanted to end my life. He wasn't really considered a very good doctor with the pupils – he seemed to offer everyone a paracetamol and an elasticated bandage for every ailment. He couldn't come up with any solution so I left as I had arrived.

I returned to lessons and during one of my classes one of the teachers poked their heads round the door. Looked around the room, saw me and then left.

I didn't think anything of it until break...

The chapel bell sounded at break time – something unheard of at school so we were all ushered into the pews. The headmaster announced solemnly that one of the boys had committed suicide by jumping in front of the London train. This boy was one of the few people who spoke to me in the boarding house – he was the person I used to turn to when the going got tough.

I was devastated.

I was dumbfounded.

My life started to spin in a blur. Why me? Why wasn't it me? Why hadn't I been brave enough to do the same? Now I was left here in this hell-hole alone.

I grieved for a long time, the whole boarding house did really – all 50 boys. We went off the rails – paying no heed to authority, graffitiing the notices and drinking lots of alcohol.

I went and hid in the woods and played truant – skipping lessons and activities. And in return mother nature helped to heal me.

At what point I decided things needed to change I am not sure but I decided to start playing sport again. My back was still painful but I could play as long as I was warmed up. That decision helped to save me really. I knew that if I was to survive boarding school then I had to start playing sport again. I had to start exercising.

And since that time I have found that exercise in whatever form has always given me a lifeline of sorts – walking, qigong, yoga, laughter yoga, dancing, boxing, martial arts. Whether feeling depressed or angry or feeling like I was losing it completely exercise has helped to lift me out of that negative space. And now I exercise because I love it. And now I exercise because of the way it makes me feel.

And when the challenging days rear their heads as they still do from time to time, exercise is one of the ways I use to lift and clear my head.

Recap on Exercise

Exercise is a phenomenal way of de-stressing. But what tips have we covered in this chapter to make exercise work for you?

- **Find an exercise you love doing** when you start your exercise routine. The more passionate you are about a sport or activity, the more you will be inspired to not only keep doing the activity going but to actually make it part of your life.

- If you have difficulty motivating yourself with exercise then a key is to **spend some time exercising with others**. This helps you to keep a routine and to be accountable when you just don't feel like it!

- Walking is such a simple activity for relieving stress that most of us don't do it now. Instead we use our cars or any reason for not walking. **Start walking as much as possible** and you will see your mind clear and your stresses released.

- **Yoga is a great form of stress relief** which has been around for thousands of years. By combining movement with deep breathing you get a physical workout and leave feeling relaxed.

- **Tai Chi and Qigong are another great way of reducing stress.** These simple Chinese exercises are designed to slow the breathing and energize the body.

- **Other forms of exercise** which are good for managing stress are running/jogging, working out in a gym, martial arts, and dancing. Any exercise which really helps you to be physical and rooted in the body helps to release tension the body has stored up through stress.

- **Swimming, especially outdoors in nature, is a wonderful way of de-stressing.**

- If you can do any of the above activities in nature, then all the better. **Being in nature** helps to ground your body and mind and it means that you are breathing in pure, clean air. Problems are more easily released when you are exercising in a stunning location.

Chapter One – Questions

1. What exercises do you love doing (if you have problems thinking of one, go back to childhood and think of an exercise you loved or one you always wanted to do)?

2. Who could you get to join you in exercising (which friends inspire and lift you and would be up for working out together)?

3. Where could you fit a walk into your day (taking the kids to school, on the way to work…)?

4. Are there any yoga, tai chi or qigong classes locally? How could you find out more about classes and set a time to do it?

5. What local parks or areas in nature do you love? When was the last time you visited? How can you fit a visit to nature into your week?

CHAPTER 2
Finances, Wealth and Money

Money can be a stress for people, especially in times of recession and economic "turmoil". If there is a common stressor among people then money is definitely up there. We seem to spend a lot of time worrying about how we are going to make ends meet and how we are going to pay the bills.

I personally grew up in a household where money was a sore point. For a period of time my family struggled to make ends meet and so my parents argued about money on a regular basis. Does this sound like a similar trend in your own life?

We give a lot of energy and focus to money and almost deify it. Is money really as important as we try to make out? And is there another way of working with money which takes away the stress and anxiety? Is there a well-being way around money?

These were all questions I asked myself as I started to earn money myself. I trained in one of the top business schools in Europe and on graduation started work in London. I wanted to get work in banking as this was where my partner was working and this was where I had worked for 6 months while on placement.

But fortunately or unfortunately I could not find work in banking. So I ended up taking a job working in sales. For those of you who have worked in sales then you will know that it is pretty hard work. In fact most of you will have come across salespeople, both men and women, calling you up to sell you anything from double glazing to a new mobile contract. It is not the most cherished form of work.

So here I was in a big multinational selling financial training courses over the phone. It was rather arduous work. I made roughly 250 calls a week and made on average 1 sale a week. If you work out the maths on that, yes , that makes up for quite a lot of rejection every week...

But after period of time, the sales started to roll in. I was selling expensive courses – some were £5000 and I was working on commission so the commissions started to roll in. And quite soon I was earning a really good wage doing this job.

And yet for the most part it was really, really stressful. I remember walking from the Blackfriars tube stop in London to my workplace psyching myself up. Deep breath – "you can do it, Piers!", deep breath "you can do it, Piers!"

I was earning great money but I started to become really disillusioned. "Is this really what I want to be doing? Is money the be all and end all of life? Because I have a whole lot of money but I have very little happiness." and looking around talking to colleagues or clients I realised that few of them had high levels of happiness. Sure, they might claim to be happy to your face but they were stressed, didn't see their families much, and didn't really do much apart from working and drinking.

I remember hearing of one lady who worked in investment banking. She was new and had only been there for a few weeks. She went to work on the Monday morning and she left on the Wednesday evening! She had to stay at work all that time and it was just expected that you drop everything for work... No sleep, no rest... work, work, work.

I saw that we placed such a lot of emphasis on money. Money was more important than health, family or happiness. It wasn't balanced and still doesn't feel balanced now. But it is changing and hopefully the words in this book will start to help you see that there is another way.

Looking back after spending 3 years in a monastery where some of the monks had not touched money for up to 40 years, I see that there is another way, maybe not to the extent as not handling money for 40 years but certainly a less intense way than the West is used to.

How do we make peace within ourselves so that money is just as it is – a useful commodity – energy essentially, rather than a heavy weight around our necks?

Over this chapter we will investigate a different way, and hopefully for you a more balanced way of being around money.

9. See The Wealth In All That You Do

We often only see the wealth that is in our banks or in our pockets. Have you ever stopped to think about the wealth that you have throughout your life?

Indeed if you look at the etymological (historical) path of the word wealth it actually comes from the root of well-being. So in fact we could really say that someone who is wealthy is one who has well-being in all areas of their life – emotional, mental, physical, sexual, financial and spiritual. In the West we look only at the financial aspects when we talk about wealth. We think that if someone has lots of money then they must be wealthy.

And yet this is often very rarely the case. The richest people financially are sometimes the poorest people in other areas – abusive relationships, poor health, emotionally empty.

A survey on US private banks in 2000 found that 64% of the participants who were worth $38 million or more felt financially insecure (the U.S. Private Bank's 2000 Study on "Wealth with Responsibility", from Deutsche Bank's Forum magazine, 6/2000, page 24). That is truly amazing – it would not seem that they are truly wealthy. They have all that money yet feel insecure. You are probably thinking to yourself, "Well, if I had that type of money I wouldn't feel financially insecure." But would you? Until we do the work in all areas of our life and truly appreciate what we have now in this moment we will probably be the same. Indeed Mariah Carey, who is worth $100 million talked about how she still feels financially insecure from time to time...

Have you ever spent time focusing on what you actually have rather than what you don't have as in the cases above?

By focusing on all that you have and are grateful for e.g. friends, good health, eyes to read with, ears to hear with, family, house over your head, lungs to breathe with and so on, you realise that you already have wealth in your life.

On the other hand, when you focus just on what you don't have then you will always not have enough. No matter how many things you buy you will always feel you don't have enough – someone else will always have something bigger and better than you.

Well, until you learn to see the wealth that you have right now and are grateful for it, you will probably find that you feel lack in some way. The following exercise will start to address that.

EXERCISE 5

Gratitude For Your Wealthy Life

1. Get a piece of paper or a journal. Write in it all the things that you are grateful for now. What inner and external wealth do you have that you can be grateful for? What is in your life that you take for granted but if it was to disappear you would really feel – heating in your house, a heart beating in your chest, children and loved ones.

2. Once you have written down 30 things that you are grateful for read through the list and really feel the positive feeling of gratitude. Let it fill you and overflow from you. Really feel how lucky you are.

3. Now imagine this feeling as a colour. Where is it located in the body? Allow the feeling to spread throughout every cell in your being. Now double the intensity of the colour. Double it again. Feel the amazing feelings racing through your body. When this feeling is at its peak press you thumbs and 2nd fingertips together and hold for 10 seconds. And then release.

4. Any time during the day that you feel yourself going into a feeling of lack or worry around money imagine your visualised colour around you, think of something you are grateful for and press your thumb and 2nd fingertips together.

5. By doing this practice on a daily basis you start to reprogram your neural pathways in your brain so that you start to draw to you more and more things to be grateful for.

Exercise 5 focuses on the positive things to be grateful for and the exercise 6 takes a different slant helping you to see that the challenges in your life and sometimes your greatest gift:

EXERCISE 6

Gratitude For The Challenging Times

1. Now think about 10 situations in your life which were quite unpleasant and you didn't enjoy e.g. my computer broke down, I broke my leg.

2. Once you have written this list then find something you are grateful for from that situation (this is a tough one but so worth it) e.g. my computer broke down but it allowed me to spend the day with my family / my computer broke down but I was then able to focus on my paperwork which I had been putting off for ages. I broke my leg and it gave me a chance to have a rest, unwind and learn all about taking it easy!

3. Once you have written them down look back at the list and start to see that whatever arises in your life can be seen in a positive light and a negative one. Guess which one is more pleasant? By focusing on the light side you create more light and wealth increasing situations.

Well done for doing these exercises. Keep repeating exercise 5 as many times as possible in a day even if it is just to stop, like now, like right now... and appreciate three things around while feeling the colour you visualised.

10. Give Away 10% Of All You Earn

Wow you must be thinking – are you crazy? I don't have any money and why on earth would I want to be giving away 10% of all I earn.

Simple...

By giving away money, you receive more in return. Most of the richest men and women in the world know this secret and that is why they are so wealthy.

There is a story in the US of a man who gave money away all his life. This was his purpose. He had a column in a newspaper and asked people to write to him with the worthiest of causes so he could help them. The interesting thing is that he started off with $2 million but over the course of his life gave away $30 million in his life time!

Doesn't make sense does it? Where did the other money come from? When you give so you receive...

It works psychologically because we become much happier and more content with money. Rather than holding on and being miserly, we allow money to flow and we become much more relaxed around money. We move into an area of trusting. Trusting that the universe will provide. This is a challenge for many people – to trust, not just other people but that this is a benevolent universe, that we will be taken care of.

"The most important question a person can ask is, 'Is the Universe a friendly place?' "

— Albert Einstein

When we do indeed feel that the universe is friendly, that we can truly trust then doors open. How does it feel to think of the universe as friendly or unfriendly? When we focus on it being friendly it becomes that way. And likewise with being unfriendly.

Another aspect of giving away 10% of all you earn is the feeling that wholehearted giving gives you. It feels wonderful. Many times in my own life when I have been most generous I have felt most happiness. I remember when I was leaving Ghana after being there for a year that I gave one of the Ghanaian employees £50 as a leaving gift. For me it was not much but for him it was 2 months salary and I believe he started crying. He wrote to me for many years after saying how grateful he was to me.

At another point when I was travelling in the north of Ghana I was speaking with a couple of European tourists who were with an African friend. This friend was saying that she couldn't afford to visit her son in another part of the country as travel was too expensive. I decided to give her £40 and she took it not knowing how much it was in the local currency Cedis. The most valuable note in Ghana was 5,000 Cedis – which was worth 50 pence. She wrote to me later saying that it really shocked her when she went to change the money and found out how much it was worth – and she bought a ticket to go and see her son...

These memories are powerful for me – how can you be generous today, even if it is just to smile at someone you don't know?

And when you give 10% of your earnings, just as the case of the philanthropist who started with $2 million, you will find wealth drawn to you. Opportunities will just avail themselves to you. The following exercise will help you to get into the flow and came from the writer Michael Losier.

EXERCISE 7

Today I Observed my Abundantness Here...

1. Get out your journal or you can do this exercise in your head (if doing in your head then read through exercise once then put the book down). Best to be done at the end of the day but any time is good.

2. Write down the following phrase, Today I Observed My Abundantness Here...

3. And write down/ think of the different areas where you have experienced abundantness e.g. The weather was glorious today, A young man gave me his seat on the bus, I got to meditate this morning, I have a really comfortable bed, My partner is so patient, I was given $300, My body was in great shape...

4. By focusing on what you are grateful for draws more to be grateful for into your life.

11. Give Without Expectation Of Return

When giving it is so important that you come from a heart overflowing with joy and abundance. When you give you must give from your heart, really feel that love and generosity overflowing from you as you give.

If you give with any sense of duty or miserly feeling then you block more wealth coming your way. In the West we give. We are good at giving – charities, donations, supporting causes, but often times we give from a sense of duty rather than from a sense of love, a sense of joy and wanting to give.

Whether this stems from our childhood of our parents feeling obliged to leave donations at church when the baskets were passed round, or feeling obliged to give

to people because everyone else is doing it is not important. What is important is unconditional giving – a pure, overflowing, joy filled giving. We give because it makes us feel good.
Indeed, as a society in the West, we give because we are expecting something in return. In the case of our parents' in church, for example, it was the respect of our fellow parishioners or lack of it thereof. We give expecting a compliment. We give at Xmas because sometimes we feel we must, or that we will receive gifts in return.

True giving is selfless giving. We give with no expectation of anything in return. We give with a completely open heart. A heart filled with joy. We give because we love to give, because it makes us feel amazing. This is unconditional giving. And of course when we give with no expectation of return... We receive true abundance flowing back to us 10 fold.

The following exercise will help to free up the abundance to start flowing more freely through your life.

EXERCISE 8

Learning To Attract Abundance Into Your Life

1. Find someone who makes your heart sing and has made such a difference in your life

2. Or find an organisation or business who has supported you and made you feel great about yourself. Maybe it's your local church or monastery, maybe it's your favourite author.

3. Make a donation only when you feel good and feel abundant and joyful. Focus on the feeling of what that person has given to you and how grateful it makes you feel. Give with that sense of joy. And you know what, the universe will hear and wealth will flow into your life.

12. Practise Giving On A Small Level To Start Off With

A lot of us find giving unconditionally to be challenging. If this is you then try out giving small at the beginning.

This is a practise that I learned when I first joined the monastery when I would go for a walk each day to the local lake. It was a 20 minute walk from the monastery and was really beautiful.

There were hundreds of ducks, swans and geese so I would take the leftover bread to the lake and feed them. It became a wonderful routine and I found it to be a really wonderful way of opening my heart to giving and learning to receive. I received a lot of joy and happiness from feeding those swans, ducks and geese.

And I got into a routine of giving. And it made my day being in nature and giving. Sure there were times when my heart wasn't open but that didn't matter as I was learning. It is better to give than not at all but it is best to learn to give from an open heart with no expectation of return.

EXERCISE 9

Learning To Give With An Open Heart

1. Go and buy yourself a loaf of bread or a bag of porridge oats and go for a walk to the local lake or river.

2. Find some ducks, geese or swans and feed them. But remember to keep your heart open and really feel how good this feels. Allow this abundance to flow through you. Feel your heart as an open vessel, flowing through your arms, into the bread and down into the birds.

3. Get to know how it feels to give and how good it feels. And press your thumb and 2nd fingertips together when the feelings are strongest.

Some of the richest people on the planet do not enjoy their wealth because they fear it. They fear losing it and fear someone else taking it. They do not understand the amazing joy and happiness it brings from giving with an open heart. It is one of the most wonderful feelings.

13. Give Out What You Want To Receive

This principle works on the basis that you give out whatever it is that you want to receive. This is a really good teaching if you are always on the end of someone else's anger or spite or gossip. What it is that you are giving out? Do you gossip about other people, do you get angry and shout at others? Do you put others down with snide remarks? Do you get angry and shout internally at yourself?

Whatever you are giving out so you will receive. Therefore this principle works with wealth. If you want to receive more money then you give away money. If you want to receive more love then you give out more love. If you want others to care for you then you have to start primarily caring for yourself and then start caring for others.

So what do you personally give out? How can we tell what we are giving out?

Look at your life and you will see that what you have in your life, is what it is that you give out. Are you already financially wealthy, spiritually rich, have loving people in your life? When you see where you are at then you can start to change. And you change by starting to give.

Another level to this as we have already said, is that you have to give without expectation of return. It's no longer, "I gave him that so he owes me!" It comes from a place of, "I give because I love giving and if anything comes back that is a bonus."

It is also important to note that the universe always gives in return, but it doesn't always come from the person you were generous to. No, it can come from anywhere. When we limit it to, "Well, he owes me, I gave him this..." Then we stop it coming from anywhere else. Indeed the universe is completely abundant:

"From abundance he took abundance and still abundance remains."

— The Upanishads

The question is, will we receive the wealth when it comes along?

14. Learning To Receive Wealth

For a lot of people receiving things is a great struggle. We have become a society where we feel we should receive little and always give to others. But there needs to be balance. As I have already stated it is important to give but only from an open and abundant heart. If we give from a place of duty and a sense of "I can't afford this but I have to give this" then we block abundance coming to us.

Why? Because when money is offered to us from friends or an unexpected source what do we do? We say no, I can't take that. We ask on one hand for wealth and abundance and then on the other hand we refuse it point blank when it is offered to us.

EXERCISE 10

How Do You Receive?

1. Write the following down in your journal. What do you do when someone gives you a wonderful compliment? What do you say? How do you feel? How do you receive it? Do you receive it at all? See how you react the next time someone compliments you.

For most of us due to our upbringing we feel we do not deserve to receive anything. What answers did you come up with for the above exercise? Do you always compliment that person in return? Well, that's not receiving that's just giving the compliment back.

A great lesson that I learned in the monastery from the Abbot was learning to receive. He used to compliment me and I used to get really annoyed. I would say,

"You're lying" (Buddhist monks are not allowed to lie...), "I don't believe you", or get really angry at him.

So after a while he stopped giving me compliments because I got so upset! I realised that I had such a poor self opinion and anything good didn't make sense to me – this inner tyrant.

So I worked on myself, I started to learn to receive myself. Now what do I mean by that? I mean that I started to allow myself to be me. That meant being angry, being hurt, being a good person and not giving myself a hard time.

And how did I achieve this? Mainly through meditation as we will learn later on. This helped me to reprogram my mind and to start to receive myself as I am. And after a bit of time the Abbot started to compliment me again and my reply? "Thank you."

So this exercise is to watch what you do the next time someone compliments you. Catch yourself and start to learn to receive.

For only once you have started to learn to receive compliments from another person can you ever receive the abundance and wealth that is waiting to flow into your life.

15. Saving 10% Of All You Earn

Another great tip most wealth management teachers talk about is saving 10% of all you earn. This technique enables you to start to have a financial cushion between you and being broke.

The trick with this technique is that whatever you earn you always put 10% of your earnings aside. But this is savings and is not to be spent.

This means that should you be really struggling you should not spend that money – that money is to be saved and not spent.

When I first came across this technique I found it quite bizarre: "Why shouldn't I spend it?" I think that I had saved a small sum over the period of a few months and was quite proud of myself.

But when an unexpected expense came up, well I used the "savings". It meant that from having a buffer zone and feeling quite confident that I could do this suddenly I was left with nothing. It was like I had sabotaged myself. I didn't feel so good. I have since learned from this experience and see how powerful a tool it is. We feel more relaxed around money because we are literally more wealthy.

What this saving of 10% does is the following:

- It invites more wealth into your life because as long as you are saving from an abundant open-hearted perspective then more money is attracted to you.
- It gives you a buffer zone so that when things really get tight you almost have this safety net which means that you will be okay. You don't use it of course but it makes you feel so much more secure.
- It makes you become aware of some of the unnecessary spending that you do. This spending can be used to save and invite more wealth into your life.
- You start to feel rich because gradually your financial wealth increases – you do have more money. What this does is raises your vibration – no longer will you work for $10 an hour but only focus on earning $100 or $1000 an hour. You start to see your added wealth and start to value yourself.

16. Asking Better Questions About Wealth

But I don't have any money I hear you saying! I can't afford anything because I have no money! Money makes me stressed!

This is another technique practised by the wealth creation and success management teachers across the world. Ask better questions.

Again when I came across this I didn't quite understand what it meant. But gradually it started to dawn on me and once I understood, wow, what a difference it has made.

What it means is that instead of saying:

- I have no money so how can I save 10%?

You change it to:

- How can I bring more wealth into my life so I can save 10%?

Can you see the difference? How does the first question make you feel? And the second?

What other ways can you start to ask better questions and use your language in a positive way?

Think of an unpleasant situation from your life. How did you react? If you said:

- This is so unfair why does it always happen to me?

Change it to:

- What can I do to change this situation?
- What can I learn from this situation?
- What is this situation trying to tell me? (maybe you're not having firm boundaries, or that you are working too hard, or that you are always looking after others and not after yourself...)

So there is wealth in your words and in your questions. You can choose to have words which bring wealth and joy or pain and misery. Which do you choose? I know that I used to choose the painful ones but now see that there is no point punishing myself – life is abundant and great fun, even if it is not always evident at times...

Great wealth questions you can ask yourself:

- How can I add to the riches I already have? (For remember riches are not just financial)
- What am I really passionate and excited about and good at that people would pay me good money for?
- What ways can I give back to the world which will bring abundance to me?
- What things can I do to add value to my existing services? (a smile, free products, great service, great products)

Ask yourself these questions now. Write them down. How do they make you feel? Good? Find your own wealth questions and start to invite abundance in today. Remember wealth starts with your thoughts and your words.

17. Be Patient When Increasing Your Wealth

Was Rome built in a day or the constitution of any country written in an hour? No.

So be patient when starting out on the road to wealth. Remember to ask the right questions and use your words in a positive way.

If something doesn't work out ask, "How can I make this better? What have I learned here?"

The difference between successful and unsuccessful people is that the successful people have failed so many more times. This doesn't make sense to most people but if you think about it the unsuccessful person stops at the first hurdle, stops with the first failure. The successful person learns from his failure and keeps going. They don't stop until they reach where they want to go.

So be patient with yourself. When you fall over, pick yourself back up again. And when you fall over again, gently pick yourself up again.

The following process will help you to speed up the process of manifesting wealth into your life. I have personally found that the below exercise brings tangible results within 30 days. What you want to manifest starts arriving within 30 days (so be very careful about what you ask for...)

EXERCISE 11

Vision Movie

1. Find out what you are passionate about. What is it that you love doing? What would you love to share with the world? What have people always said that you were talented at? What relationships would you like to have? How do you want your physical health to be? What belongings would you like to manifest?

2. Start to imagine what that would look and feel like. Start to live that life. Close your eyes now and feel what it would feel like to take a holiday every month, lying on the beach sunning yourself, swimming in azure seas, living the life of your dream.

3. Go onto an internet image search engine on the computer and start to search for images which resonate with you. Save them on the desktop or in a personal separate folder called "Vision Board". Look through the different areas of your life: friends, house, holidays, activities, belongings, cars, wealth, physical health, family, financial, relaxation, relationships, career, emotional health, spiritual goals... . Save these images into your folder.

4. Be excited, be joyful in this process. What do you love doing? Going onto Google will really help in the creative process. It will get the creative juices flowing, buzzing around your system. What inspires you, lifts you, makes you feel amazing?

5. Once you have a good amount of inspirational images, open a video editing software like Windows Movie Maker. Import the files from your "Vision Board" folder. Place the pictures on the time line at the bottom.

6. Import some of your most favourite and uplifting music. Add captions on the film in the present tense of things you would like: "I am becoming more and more energized with life. I am becoming more financially abundant. I am attracting great financial wealth to me. I have amazing relationships. I am filled with joy at this amazing life. My heart is overflowing with love."

7. Then create a film to save onto your computer or burn it to a DVD.

8. Watch this film every day and where possible twice a day at least for 30 days. You might notice some differences within a few days but within 30 days of doing this process you will notice a huge shift start to come over you. Feel inspired and joyful when watching this film – dance if you want to, and watch the magic start to unfold in your life.

18. Focus On Your Own Wealth Rather Than That Of The Whole World

In times of recession a lot of people are stifled by fear. They become the recession. Every article you read or program you see on TV talks about the recession.

But my advice to you is not to focus on that, not to even go there. I personally do not read newspapers, or watch the news. Recession, sensationalization and misery sells. Remember that when you buy a newspaper. They have every interest in telling you how bad it is because they are going to sell more units. Doesn't seem fair really but this is how the world can be. There is lots of abundance out there – but it doesn't shift newspaper units so doesn't appear in the press or news. But it is out there I assure you.

So focus on your own wealth, on the abundance that is coming to you in every breath you breathe, and every step you take. Don't worry about what is happening in the rest of the world – remember it is not the "true" reality anyway – it's just what sells newspapers – there a whole lot of prosperous people out there too.

If you can avoid talking about how bad the economy is then do so. If you can avoid reading all the negative reports and focus on some positivity in your life all the much better.

We are what we think about.

So think wealthy thoughts and abundant dreams! Watching your Vision Movie will help you immensely with this. Rather than filling your mind with the images others are choosing to place there – lack, recession, poverty, war... you start to play your own TV with your Vision Movie – love, abundance, joy, peace, money, more than enough for everyone...

When you spend your days watching TV telling you how bad it is then you pre-pave, you prepare more of what you are watching – what you focus on you receive more of. So by watching your Vision Movie instead you start to prepare a very different path for yourself. One of abundant, light, love and pleasure. Which do you want to choose? Make the choice now.

I always had a strange perception around money and wealth as a child. At the age of 5, my father, who had been a naval officer until that time, had cirrhosis of the liver and was invalided from the Navy.

From that period on money became very tight in our household. My father spent a year in and out of hospital, very close to death, as I was to learn later on. My mother took care of the household and worked all hours to earn money to keep the household going. We would visit my father in the local hospital and go up to London to visit him there when he was transferred.

When my father recovered from his illness he spent a period of time unemployed. He was now tee-total but would still have huge bouts of rage. In the end he started up his own business. He began to sell printed t-shirts and pencils and did engraving work. He joined up with a shoe repair man and opened a shop up in the centre our local town.

My father worked really hard and yet he really hated that job: spending his days in a small room with noisy machines, glue smells and boredom. His dream, as I was to learn later on, was to find a plot of land and start a small holding. It was only later in his life did he find that, but due to his work had very little time to spend there. It was only when he was diagnosed with terminal cancer did he stop working. His last 6 months alive were spent solely at his smallholding with his partner.

I went to help out with my father and his partner in those last 6 months. I had by that point just left London and was living with my sister an hour south of the big city. I had taken a job doing temporary work for an international telephone company. I was inputting data from the phone repairs which came to the factory. I was finding the work really tedious – the same bits of information being inputted every 15 minutes, but it gave me the freedom to take time off when I needed.

So every few weeks I would take time off for a week and go and help out. It was a wonderful reawakening going to spend time on the small holding. I was going through my first breakdown/ breakthrough at the time. Everything in my life had fallen away within a few months – my long-term partner, my lovely apartment next to Hampstead Heath, my job, my friends... But the time spent at my father's smallholding, in nature, being of service gave me some respite.

I had spent the last 5 years living and working in London trying to live out the "Dream" - good job, good salary, drinking at the right places... But I felt hollow inside. Surely there was more to life than this. Surely there was more to making money and a career than this. And in some strange way, there on the smallholding I started to reawaken that within myself. There is something more to City life. The gentle rhythm and silence of the countryside embedded a sense of stillness within me. Yes, there was another way.

And yet in some bizarre twist I wasn't really much help on the smallholding. I wasn't particularly fit having sat on a chair most of the previous 5 years. And I didn't really know what I was doing. And my father? He really disliked me being there. He was a really active and proactive man and he couldn't do anything any more. I felt that for him, with me being there it was humiliating. He was gruff and short with me so I kept out of his way. His partner was appreciative of me being there so I liaised with her.

On one of my stays I realised that my father didn't have long to live, maybe a few days. I asked to speak with him. He was perched on a single bed, propped up against the wall, his body crumpled by the effects of cancer. I told him that I felt that he hated me his whole life. He was shocked by this and broke down into tears. He said that it wasn't true. He said that his whole life had been a lie, that he had lived a lie. He had been in institutions all his life having left boarding school at 16 to go straight into the Navy. It seemed to me that he hadn't done anything that he wanted, not until 6 months from his death. He felt happy now that he had found his new partner and was living on his smallholding, but it was too late. It was much too late.

And a few days later he did die. It felt good that for the first time in my life I had a honest talk with him. It was just a shame it took so long to come.

What a powerful lesson it was, to see my father living his whole life as a lie. How many of us have watched our parents living lies to please society, family, peers? And on what level has this gone into us? Are we living a lie? Are you living a lie? Are you waiting until you get sick before you make the step to do what you want? Start now, start today. Life is worth living, life is abundant but we have to start to want to choose life now, to choose to do what feeds us, rather than what is expected of us.

Are you waiting for something before you start to choose life – sickness, the death of a loved one, redundancy, divorce? Wait no longer, choose life today.

Recap on Finances, Wealth and Money

This is a powerful topic. Money can be one of the greatest stressors we have in life. What have we covered in this chapter?

- By focusing on what you do not have only increases your worry. **Start to learn to see what wealth you already have in your life**, e.g. your good health, your relationships, the roof over your head. By doing this you fill yourself with wonderful feelings and attract more wealth into your life.

- **By giving away 10% of all you earn** to charities or people who have really inspired you, you help to make yourself feel really good about money. It feels so good to give to others from an open heart. And by allowing money to flow out easily, you allow more money to flow in.

- When giving one must **give out of the pure joy and love** – as soon as it becomes a duty then don't do it. Find someone who has really inspired you and give to them.

- A lot of us don't give because we feel we don't have the money to give. Well, start small – **give of yourself**: a smile, a helping hand, positive thoughts and prayers, but make sure you give with an overflowing heart.

- **If you want to receive more money then give away money**, if you want more love then give out more love to the world. Look around you, see that the richest are most often the most generous, e.g. Bill Gates giving away $5 billion and Warren Buffet giving away $37 billion. And the most loving are those who shower the world with love e.g. The Dalia Lama, Mother Theresa

- When you start to **learn to receive wealth** then the doors of the universe open themselves up to you. A lot of us ask for wealth but then when our friends or family offer to give us money – we decline it. Start to receive what you ask for.

- **Save 10% of all you earn** – a great way of starting to attract wealth and abundance to you.

- **Ask better questions** when it comes to wealth and abundance. "What can I learn from this mistake? What talents do I have that others would be willing to pay me for?" How can I create more wealth in my life and in those of others?"

- **Be patient when creating new wealth and opportunities** in your life. Everything arrives in its right time, your job is to focus on what you want, to work towards it but also to let go and trust that it is coming to you.

- It is very easy in times of recession to get pulled in by the media and news about how bad it is. Don't go there. **Focus on the wealth that you have in your life** – from being able to read this, to having a healthy family. By focusing on the negative, life becomes pretty depressing. Turn it around by focusing on the joy in your life.

Chapter Two – Questions

1. List 20 things that you are grateful for in your life.

2. List 3 establishments or people who have inspired you or filled you with joy and love. Choose one and make a donation to this organization or person.

3. List 5 occasions that you have been generous in your life and given to others. How does that make you feel?

4. Write down any negative internal dialogues you have about money and wealth. Change these negative blurts into positive affirmations (e.g. I'm always broke, to, I'm attracting abundance into my life.)

5. Name 5 areas in your life where you are truly wealthy e.g. physically, mentally, spiritually, relationally, financially…

CHAPTER 3

Using Spirituality To Meet The Challenges in Life

What is spirituality? **Spirituality can be any form of practice which feeds you on a deep level.** In understanding everything is spiritual in its basis. So any practice which feeds you is spiritual. This can be going for a walk in nature, spending time with uplifting friends, meditating or doing tai chi. It can be an organized religions like Buddhism, Christianity or Islam.

The 20th century philosopher Pierre Teilhard De Chardin said that:

> ***"We are not human beings having a spiritual experience but spiritual beings having a human experience."***

Spirituality is our lifeblood as humans. Essentially, everything that we do based on the above quote, is spiritual. Puts a different spin on how we perceive doing the washing up or weeding the garden. My understanding is that practices which make us feel good and feed us help us to connect to this idea that we are spiritual beings.

In the study of Quantum Physics one comes to the realisation that everything is made of the same thing – energy. In the film *The Secret* one of the teachers uses the example that if you were to ask a scientist to describe this energy, they would say – it always has been, it always will be, it can never be created or destroyed, it is always flowing into form, through form and out of form.

If you were to ask a priest what their definition of God is they would probably say, - He has always been, He always will be, He can never be created or destroyed, He is always flowing into form, through form and out of form.

Yes, they are the same.

I came from a Christian background and growing up I had to attend church up to 5 times a week. I felt very disconnected from the church and the teachings. It was just boring to a young boy. The idea of this powerful, angry, aggressive, punitive, distant God didn't appeal to me unsurprisingly. In fact, this image just reminded me of my own father.

At the age of 14 I went on a Christian holiday and in some ways found God. My friend had just died and I was still feeling suicidal, but somehow the prayers and the people helped to lift and shift me.

But on return to school I quickly became disillusioned with Christianity and God. I found the priests at school to be hypocritical, they said one thing in the sermon and practised something completely different in their everyday lives. I was taken advantage of by one of the priests after showing him my vulnerability and that was it. No more visits to the priest – I wasn't going to trust them again.

And I started to hate God. I started to blame "Him" for all my ills and problems. In some ways it helped to have someone to blame for the pain I was experiencing.

The hatred slowly filtered inside and I no longer thought about or talked about God. I didn't believe in Him. "There you go, I take my power back – you have no control over me". And this is the way it stayed for many years. I helped out with Christian charities and attended services, but always found the Christians I met to be hypocritical. They preached one thing and practised another. It seemed that to get to God I had to go through them or through the church. It seemed like they were spiritual salespeople – trying to get me to buy their form of Christianity. So I kept my distance denying that God existed at all.

And then the most curious thing happened. I had been staying in the Buddhist monastery for a few weeks when the Abbot gave a talk and in it he spoke about Devas. "What are Devas?" I asked someone later on. "Angels, heavenly beings." I was shocked. "You mean they exist?" "Of course," they replied.

So I started to research and to my great surprise there in the Buddhist scripture were references to angels, spirits and God – Brahma. Indeed, the Buddha is said to have spent a rains retreat (a period of a few months) in the heavenly realms himself.

I didn't know what to think to start off with. Here I was in a Buddhist monastery and the monks and the scriptures were quite clearly saying that there was a God. It was rather matter of fact – there is a God. And one of the precepts of a Buddhist monk is to not lie. And yet here they were saying that God existed. For the first time I began to believe that there might be a God. I mean the Buddhists weren't trying to sell me anything to do with God or Christianity. They were just saying God exists, but Buddhists don't follow "Him" or Jesus' teachings.

I mulled this over for a period of time. And the more time I stayed in the monastery the more it became a revelation for me – wow, there IS actually a God. Amazing. Incredible.

At this point I didn't leave the monastery to follow the teachings of Christianity again, but my perception that there was no God changed completely. I found God in a Buddhist monastery. An interesting concept.

Now, for you what is your own connection to your own spiritual truth? Do you still hold anger or hatred toward a distant, and oppressive God? Or do you hold a connection on a different level through being in nature or to your own spiritual path?

This chapter will explore what tools there are for connecting to that spirit, that life-force within you. This chapter will help you to unearth, reconnect, remember or refresh your own version of your spirituality.

Having a spiritual practise is powerful. Just as De Chardin said that we are spiritual beings having a human experience, so being spiritual in whatever way that is for us, is part of us. It is so important.

And this doesn't necessarily mean you have to follow a specific religion. No, as has been said before this could mean spending time on your own, walking in nature, writing poetry or stories. This can be spirituality as well.

For me spirituality is connecting to your heart, connecting to the love and beauty that resides in all of us. And there are many ways of doing this. We will look at some of these over the course of this chapter.

19. Investigate The Spirituality That You Are Interested In

A lot of people spend their days running away from what they don't want: past jobs, past friendships, past relationships. And the same goes for spirituality. In my generation in the UK, a lot of us had to go to church or Sunday school even if we didn't want to. There wasn't a choice whether we wanted to or not, or whether we believed or not.

So as far as spirituality goes we know what we don't want – we don't want to be forced into a church, religion, or spirituality against our wills. And so what do we do? We run from these things.

As you will find out later in my own personal story, I often found friends, colleagues and lovers would run a mile at the word "spirituality", or "religion". They would look at me with disdain at the mention of the above words.

Maybe you are in the same position – this concept bothers you or you are just not that interested.

I know I never felt I was.

And yet once I started to investigate what was out there other than my own negative experiences I found a huge wealth of information and tools that really worked for me.

Once I started to work out what "I" wanted things shifted and I was drawn to some amazing spiritual resources and experiences. The following exercise will help you to work out what you want:

EXERCISE 12

Finding Out What You Are Interested In Spiritually

1. Now here's a task. Go to your average bookshop or a new age store and find the new age book section.

2. Close your eyes.

3. Ask to be guided to the book which jumps out at you, the book which you need the most in your life.

4. Open your eyes and see what you see. Feel what you feel – maybe it is calm, resistance, whatever it is, let it be. And watch the voices, "Oh that's not what I want!" And let them be. One book or other will pull you, attract you.

5. What jumps out at you? What appeals to you? What is the book or subject that you've always wanted to read or learn about but have never got round to it?

6. And when your inner critic kicks in and says, "Oh, you don't want to buy that… I've heard that's rubbish…etc." Ignore it, go with your intuition. Usually when the inner critic kicks in is a sign that you are definitely on the right track!

7. And you'll find in your hand a magical book exactly in the area that you need. It works every time even if you don't believe it!

The reason I recommend this in a bookshop and not online is that online we can get so distracted, so confused. I want this exercise to be one connected to the heart rather than the mind.

20. Living an Upright and Upstanding Life

All the religions that I have studied teach this very simple rule. Live a life that is upstanding, just and kind. Treat others how you would like to be treated yourself. And I would add one in, treat yourself as you would like others to treat you.

The amount of worry I used to feel because of things I had said, done or thought about was huge. I so enjoyed being free of that worry in the monastery. It felt so good.

I lived by 8 precepts which basically said that: I should not kill, should not take what is not given, should not take intoxicants, should refrain from any sexual act, should refrain from using entertainments, sleep mindfully (not oversleep) and have mindful speech – being careful what I said.

This really helped to take away worry about how I was acting. I didn't have to think – I shouldn't have said that, I shouldn't have done that or I shouldn't have taken that.

At the beginning of my time in the monastery I realised that I was really bad at "borrowing" things and not giving them back and taking things "presuming" it would be okay.

But I soon realised that as a society we believe that it is okay to take what is not ours. And this is very much fear based. We fear that we do not have enough so we need to take from others. I have heard from people that, you should never pay for anything from big companies because they have too much money already!

By doing this you add fear into your life that you will get caught. And of course, this leads to stress. Why have this hanging over you when to live an upright life, which every spiritual teacher will tell you, is a way of true happiness?

Ask before taking something. It sounds stupid on one level, but on another it is respectful. We presume to know that it is all right without getting the okay from the other person. Resentment can build up and more stress. Ask for clarity if someone says you don't need to ask every time - "Is it okay if I take this whenever I want?"

To clarify this and communicate this means that there are no misunderstandings. As a society, certainly in Britain, we have this misnomer that it is okay to take from certain establishments or businesses. How many times have you taken glasses from pubs or bars? How many times have you taken stationery from the company you work in? I know I used to do it all the time.

But what we are left with is a feeling gnawing inside of ourselves. We deny these feelings by distracting ourselves or keeping ourselves busy or telling ourselves it is okay. These feelings still remain inside of ourselves – we just don't acknowledge them. But when we stop taking what is not given the relief is amazing. When I personally stopped taking what was not mine in the monastery, it felt lovely. One less thing to worry about.

Become aware of your habits. Do you take what is not yours? Do you take money from your spouse without checking beforehand? Do you read their emails or texts without asking if it is okay? These are all forms of taking what is not given.

What I am suggesting here is not that you give yourself a hard time for doing this. No, what is being suggested is that you become aware of what you are doing. Once you are aware of what you are doing then you can do something to change it. There is no judgement here. We live in a society where it has become acceptable to take what is not ours. We have been told it's okay. But look in your heart. How does it feel to know you might be caught or that what you are doing is not really right? I know that for me it didn't feel good at all.

So investigate this. Look at this and check it out. What are my habits – judgement free? Feel how it feels to be doing this.

One of the first things to look at is would I feel comfortable telling someone about what I have taken? How would my partner feel if she knew I was looking at his/her private texts? Or how would my manager feel if they knew I was taking company stationery?

Investigate and see what you come up with. By learning to refrain from taking what is not yours a stress drops away from you and you move along the well-being way.

21. Refraining From Killing Living Things

The Buddhist teacher Ajahn Brahamvamso (Brahm) often talks about the 5 Buddhist precepts which are practised by lay practitioners across the world. Every new moon and full moon and on certain festival days the lay people will request and recite these 5 precepts. These 5 precepts are very similar to the 8 precepts I have spoken about before:

- Refrain from killing any living being
- Refrain from using intoxicants
- Refrain from lying or gossiping – mindful speech
- Refrain from taking what is not given
- Refrain from sexual misconduct

How Ajahn Brahm puts it, is that if you can't do all 5 precepts then try 4, if not 4, then try 3, if not 2 then just don't kill anyone... His message is to be relaxed around the precepts. By giving ourselves a hard time for not sticking to the precepts precisely we just add to our stress and anxiety.

The precept about not killing things is a powerful one. I remember when I was helping out at my father's smallholding when he was sick. They were having problems with moles and because they were organic were using traps rather than chemicals to catch the moles.

I was in the garden with my father's partner. She asked me to check the mole traps. Inside was a mole. It moved. My father's partner flinched and said something along the lines that I would need to kill it. I was resistant to this but took the mole away to the bonfire.

I crouched down and held the mole in my left hand. I took a trowel in my other hand and tried to hit it but felt horror at doing this. I felt devastated (I am crying as I write this now). The first blow didn't kill it so I had to hit it again. Blood trickled down its head and it stopped moving. I started to cry uncontrollably. I couldn't believe that I had killed something. It felt terrible. I vowed then that I would never do that again... To take life is an absolutely horrible feeling.

In Buddhism they say that when we kill we close a part of our heart off. Even if it is "just" to kill a fly or a wasp. I feel that our job in our life is to open our hearts and to do things to keep them that way.

As I have studied since my monastic days I have seen that the Native Americans connect with the soul of the animal before they kill it. They teach only to take that which is offered and give thanks once the animal has given of itself. It is done with an open heart. And in return the animal lets go of struggling. In the West we rarely do this – we kill without thinking. Do you slap your hands together when a fly goes past or tread on a spider when it runs on the floor? Be aware of your actions. When you are aware of what you are doing and you feel the consequences then the heart wants to find a different way.

And as with taking what is not given, another stress and anxiety falls away. Your life becomes more peaceful and at ease. You start to really cherish the life around you and the life within you.

22. Being Gentle and Kind With Your Words

Often times in the hurly burly of modern day living we say things that we just don't mean.

Have you ever done this? Have you ever got into a fight with a partner because you said something out of line? Have you ever said something that later on you regretted? Have you ever said anything which cost you a friendship or a job?

Mindful speech is important in Buddhism and is also really important for choosing wellness and relieving stress in your life. Wouldn't it be nice not to have that conflict because of something you said? Wouldn't it be nice to not be worrying and stressed out because of something you said?

Well this is what mindful speech is all about. But what is it exactly?

A breakdown of mindful speech can be seen as the following:

- The art of reflecting before you speak
- Finding the right time to say things
- Saying those things in a way which comes from a kind and compassionate place within yourself
- Asking yourself whether you can refrain from saying something. If you can't then don't say it because it is not coming from a kind place. Usually it will be coming from a place of anger and fear and will come across as such.

- Not indulging in gossip (how do you feel when you hear people talking behind your back?)
- Bringing beauty and grace to the world through your words not pain and suffering.

There is a story of a Buddhist monk who was living in community. Something happened between himself and another – a misunderstanding. This Buddhist monk wanted to find the right time to speak to the second person. So he waited. And he waited. And he waited. As the story goes the monk waited years and years before he found the right time to speak.

Now personally I feel that years and years can be too long, but in some cases it is best to wait before speaking, and for a period of time. We wait until we are settled and calm within ourselves before we speak to another. For when we approach another when we are angry, frustrated or annoyed, the other person does not hear our words but feels them. And they react accordingly – in anger, frustration, or annoyance. And an argument ensues.

When on the other hand we take care of our emotions first – we calm ourselves down, we get into a happier space, then we can communicate and in most cases the other party will hear us. The following exercise will help with this.

EXERCISE 13

Mindful Speaking

1. You find yourself in a conversation. Before speaking, breathe into your heart. This means imagine your breath being breathed into the centre of your chest when you breathe in. And when you breathe out relax the heart.

2. When you start to speak keep this breathing going. Imagine that you are talking from your heart. And sometimes it will feel that you shouldn't say anything or that to say a certain thing will cause grief and suffering so you refrain from doing it.

3. The good thing about this exercise is that you feel very clearly how it feels to say good and bad things. You feel the consequences. You feel how the good and beautiful things elate your heart. And you feel how the gossip and vindictive comments hurt you.

The art of reflecting before speaking is so important. If you practise meditation you will find that the meditation helps with this. You will find that you are not drawn in to speaking out of line or harshly.

Due to the fast pace of the world we sometimes don't think before we speak. A way of preventing this is if you are not sure about what you are going to say then don't say it, or give yourself time to think.

I find that if someone asks me to do something and I am not sure of the answer (or I don't get an internal "Yes!" straight away) then I say I'll have a think about it. By allowing time, the right answer comes to me and I know what to say.

So don't feel that you have to give answers straight away or be drawn into discussions or gossip if you don't want to.

21. Be Compassionate

The literal meaning of compassion is "with passion". This means that we care for others with passion, we feel what others feel and through feeling their discomfort or pain we open our hearts and help.

I have found in my own life that when I have connected to someone's humanness and suffering – seeing that they too hurt and are probably hurting greatly to have hurt me, then my heart melts. I cannot project hatred or anger at them.

I find that if I connect to someone's inner child – seeing the little boy or girl stood in front of me hurt and in pain, I am unable to feel ill will towards them. My heart melts and I usually cry later on because I feel how much they truly hurt inside.

And it is compassion that the Tibetan Buddhist monks use when they are persecuted in China. It is compassion that radiates from every pore of the Dalai Lama's body – you only need to see a photo of him to understand this.

So if you have conflict or stressful situations with someone in your life, imagine that person as a small hurt child. Imagine yourself in that person's shoes, what their life is like. And your heart will melt. I can feel my heart melting as I write this.

A further exercise you can do is as follows:

EXERCISE 14

An Exercise For Compassion: Tonglen

Tonglen is a Tibetan practise which helps to deal with stressed people and stressful situations. There is a wonderful Tibetan Buddhist teacher called Pema Chodron and she teaches Tonglen. The idea is that you breathe in others' pain and breathe out love and compassion.

The idea behind this is that as soon as you feel someone else's discomfort and pain you can only feel compassion and caring for them. Try this exercise at home to start off with, imaging the challenging situation or a challenging situation from the past. When you are faced with a similar situation you are then ready to cope with it:

1. You are confronted with a difficult situation or person; they are angry, stressed or anxious.
2. Imagine your heart is a bright luminous sphere. As you consciously breathe in, imagine that you are taking on this person's anger, toxins, or difficulty like a gray cloud. This cloud then dissolves in the bright light of your heart without leaving any trace.
3. You then breathe out a white light of love, compassion, joy and equanimity while wishing the person well. Say under your breath, "I truly wish you to be free of pain, suffering and discomfort".
4. Then do the same for the whole world. Seeing your heart as a bright luminous sphere and as you consciously breathe in, imagine that you are taking on the world's anger, toxins, or difficulty like a gray cloud. This cloud then dissolves in the bright light of your heart without leaving any trace.
5. You breathe out healing and light to all beings.

It really is very simple and you will find your heart opening in joy and love rather than closing down in fear and pain. Try it now and see how well it works. Think of someone in pain and do it for them because you don't have to be stood next to the person to do this exercise.

22. Being Gentle and Kind With Your Actions

Another key component and foundation of a spiritual practise is learning to be gentle and kind with your actions. What does this mean? It means that you take care to do all in your power to be kind, all in your power to be gentle. This means with each action reflecting, until you get used to it, I am benefiting all beings by doing this.

This could also mean doing positive actions like making someone a cup of tea, or opening a door for someone, or giving a wonderful gift. Or it could mean helping out at a charity with each action being mindful of what you do before you do it rather than rushing or racing to do something – be gentle, be kind.

Being gentle and kind with your actions will require, at the beginning, that you stop and reflect, asking the question, "Is this action for the highest good for all involved?" And that means you as well – is it for your highest good?

In the West we currently work on autopilot doing things we've always done, in the way we've always done them, at a breakneck speed. And we as a society are suffering the consequences of this lack of reflection, this lack of being gentle and kind with our actions. Look at how we have treated the earth?
By reflecting before you do something you engage and connect with a different essence; a part of you with a beating heart and a very clear understanding of how your actions will affect you emotionally.

We seem to be all or nothing in the West. We crash around without thinking and make mistakes on the one hand and then beat ourselves up and give ourselves a hard time on the other hand. For example, we get angry at our partners because we've had a bad day at work , and then beat ourselves up when our partners get upset.

Being gentle and kind with your actions means that when this is not an option, because you are so wound up, instead you go off and do something to lift you or shift how you are feeling (use any of the exercises in this book). That could be walking, singing, dancing, swimming, working out and so on. You change how you feel.

And when you feel better you can then follow through with kind and gentle actions. You create your own reality. It is clear when you look at it from this perspective – for example, you take care of how you feel, are gentle with your actions and your relationship flourishes. Or your ignore what you are feeling, shout at your clients and you then lose your income stream. Cause and effect essentially.

This does not mean that you put a happy face on it. No, you acknowledge where you are at and through a process like meditation, as you will see later on in this chapter, you allow this emotion to be. And by doing that you will find that slowly over time these emotions, which have been like a tightly wound spring up until this point, will slowly uncoil. It takes a little time, but eventually this emotion is released.

STEP ONE

Is to acknowledge where you are at. Rather than blindly bulldozing through life and wondering why you create unpleasant things. Stop, reflect, how do I feel?

STEP TWO

Is shift yourself into a better feeling space by doing something which lifts you.

STEP THREE

Is then acting from this gentle and kind space.

23. Learning to Receive Yourself Now (Don't Judge Yourself or Judge Others)

We have a strange habit in the West. We judge. We judge others but most of all we judge ourselves.

We give ourselves such a hard time. We shouldn't be like this, we shouldn't have said that, we are so useless...

But the interesting thing is, is that a lot of these judgements don't actually come from us. As children we have reasonably clean slates and minds – we are very open to others' suggestions.

A lot of these judgements about people, nations, religions, beliefs all come from somewhere. They are not truly what we feel or think. We have been told this is right and so have believed it. This might have come from friends, family, society, political leaders, or religious leaders.

Where these judgements come from doesn't matter, what matters is whether you allow your life to be ruled by them. Start to challenge your judgements. Are they true? If you believe that all money is evil, or wealthy people are criminals, for example, where did it come from? Is this true? Do you really believe this?

A judgement is taking a position against someone or something, e.g. all people who drink strong beer are alcoholics. We don't know this so we can start to challenge our judgements.

And when it comes to yourself, be aware of when you are judging yourself, "I'll never be rich, I never have wealth, I'll never be happy, I'll never be free of stress". And challenge this; look at it. Is this true? Where did this come from? Who told me this?

I remember in my own case that I thought I couldn't paint. I could hear this, "You can't paint!" in my head. When I started to challenge this I realised that this was the voice of an art teacher when I was 9 years old! I had believed him and it wasn't till I was 25 did I start painting again. I can paint, but this judgement was stopping me from picking up the brush. Once I had challenged this I could start painting again and using it as an amazing tool for wellbeing.

One part of letting go of judgements is starting to receive yourself as you are. We always have this feeling we should be otherwise: we should be 10 kilos lighter, we should be richer, we should have children, we should be better parents...

But the truth is that you will never be happy with yourself until you start to love what you are now, until you start to receive yourself as you are now. Essentially this is learning to be present. The following exercise will help you to release some of these judgements.

EXERCISE 15

Learning to Receive Yourself As You Are

1. Place your hand over your heart and say this to yourself now, "I receive myself as I am." Breathe in and out. "I am doing okay."
2. Now go through different areas of your life using this phrase as an example:
   I am ... (80 kilos) and I receive myself
   I do get ... (angry at people sometimes) and I receive myself all the same
   I don't like... (myself some of the time/ people who are late/when my husband does ...) – well I receive that as well
   I feel... (stressed) and I receive that too
   I feel... (happy, joyful, relaxed) and I receive myself for feeling that.
3. Breathe in and out and relax your shoulders.

And the interesting thing is, is that once you receive yourself in this moment, there's no struggle. You don't have to be anywhere, be any different, change anything... no everything is just perfect now.

And once you receive yourself as you are then that is when the wonderment of the universe spills itself into your life. It sees that you can receive yourself and so it gives you more wonderful things to receive!

I receive myself as I am now.
Whatever is happening in my life I receive now.

24.The Power of Meditation

Meditation is one of the most powerful tools I recommend to people who are interested in self-growth, self-improvement and self-development.

Meditation is, for me, the tool of choice for well-being and stress management. It works on so many levels and has such broad benefits that it can literally affect all areas of your life: from sleep to work, from relationships to family life. Some of the benefits are as follows:

- It reduces your CO2 consumption
- Slows the heart rate down
- Increases muscle relaxation
- Improves concentration
- Helps you to sleep
- Improves memory and creativity
- Practised regularly meditation helps to combat depression, reduce hypertension and relieve anxiety
- It helps to reduce migraines and stress headaches
- Blood circulation increases
- It has a significant effect on the way the brain works – during meditation the brain produces a balanced pattern of alpha and theta brainwaves which are some of the most relaxed and happy brainwaves the mind can go into.

Many tests have been done over the years both by scientists and doctors. The results as shown above are always impressive. Meditation is like exercise for the mind. In the same way you would exercise physically to get fit so you meditate to have a fit mind. What is a fit mind? Being able to remember things clearly, improve concentration, happier and healthier mental states and a more positive outlook on life. To have a fit body you would exercise regularly – 4 or 5 times a week for at least 30 minutes to an hour depending on age. Meditation is very similar – meditate once and you will get a little benefit; meditate twice a day for 30 minutes 4 or 5 times a week and you will see huge shifts in your life.

Routine, as I found out in the monastery, is so important in the practise of meditation. A regular routine meditating twice a day, for example, means that you meditate whatever you feel like, whatever the weather. This means that your practise deepens and becomes strong. You get insights by keeping a regular routine going. By having a routine it means that when you don't feel so good and you don't really want to meditate you do it anyway. I feel lazy... and I meditate. I feel bored... and I meditate. I feel good... and I meditate. Just as you brush your teeth twice a day come rain or shine so with routine meditation becomes an easy regular practise.

Meditation is also, as we have looked at earlier in this chapter, a space to allow emotions to be. Whatever you are feeling is acknowledged without judgement, "I feel this...." And by doing this the emotions you have been holding in your body, sometimes as aches and pains, sometimes as sickness, can start to melt away from the body.

I first learned to meditate in about 1997. I was searching for how to meditate and spent a period of a few months looking for different books and articles on how to meditate. There were books on the benefits of meditation, what you could get out of meditation but I could find no book which stated "This is how you meditate." I felt a bit frustrated really and being at business school at the time meant that I didn't know anyone who meditated or had a spiritual practise.

It seemed to me that everyone knew how to meditate but no one was telling anyone how to do it. It seemed to me that it was presumed that everyone could already meditate and therefore there was no need to teach it to others.

So this frustrated me for a while. I decided to go to the Mind, Body, Spirit Festival in King's Cross in London. I thought I am bound to find out how to meditate here.

I looked at the program and there was this talk on Transmission Meditation. I thought that must be it.

I walked in with my partner of the time who was a banker. We sat down in a room full of people and waited to see what happened. A man came on and started to show us a video. It didn't seem to have anything to do with meditation, more about a new spiritual leader. We left half way through.

How am I going to learn meditation, I thought. While walking around the stalls in the festival hall I was telling one of the stall holders that I wanted to learn meditation. He said, have you got a few minutes? I said, okay.
So we sat down on the floor in the middle of this teeming hall and he proceeded to teach me meditation. It was very simple and didn't take long at all.

After all the searching all I needed to do was ask! I have had many meditation teachers since then so have improved my practice since my time on the hall floor in King's Cross!

And in my own life meditation makes such a difference to me. When something comes up for me, like a dispute in my family, when I meditate I usually let go of it. My mind can settle and what I was worrying about falls away from me.

I remember that when I was working in the corporate environment, if I hadn't meditated in the morning then I was more likely to get bothered by things - comments or workloads. Whereas on the days where I had meditated things went more smoothly, if I did have an issue I was so much less likely to get drawn in.

So if there is one thing you take away from this book then let it be meditation.

EXERCISE 16

How To Meditate

What you need: Find a quiet place to meditate. In your bedroom or somewhere you will not be disturbed. Turn off your phones and ask family members not to disturb you (this is why it is best to be done just after waking and just before going to bed).

Posture: It is best to be sat in an upright chair so that your back is straight. You can meditate lying down but there is a chance you might fall asleep. It is best not to fall asleep but it is quite okay if you do. You can also sit cross legs on the floor or in lotus position if this feels comfortable and easy.

Time: I find the best time to meditate is in the morning first thing and in the evening last thing at night. Set your alarm for 10 minutes before you usually get up and meditate for this time.

How long?
I suggest you meditate for 10 minutes to start with twice a day and then increase that to 20 minutes once or twice a day.

How To?

1. Get comfortable. Take 3 deeps breaths. Relaxing the body as you breathe. Close your eyes if it feels comfortable to you.
2. Start to watch your breath coming in and out of your nostrils. Feel the sensations as the breath enters and leaves the body.
3. Feel the sensation of the body moving as you breathe in and out. Feel the stomach rise and fall as you breathe in and out.
4. Slow your breathing down and relax.
5. Keep focusing on the sensation of the body breathing. These sensations are your meditation object. You can also use watching a candle, listening to meditation music or use a mantra (a word) like peace, or relax which you repeat over and over, as your mediation object.

What To Do When Your Mind Wanders:
This is a normal part of meditation. The mind does wander. Each time you start to go over your shopping list or thinking about something else, just bring your mind back to your meditation object – and bring it back with kindness and gentleness.

There might be times when you meditate when you don't remember to focus on your meditation object at all. That is fine. The meditation was still a success because you sat for the 10 minutes. Keep going because you are still getting all the health benefits from meditation even if you don't feel the mind is still.

This is really, really important – even if you don't feel your mind is still, keep practising every day. After a few days or after a week you will start to notice a huge difference. Your mind will be calmer and you will be less likely to get drawn into unpleasant situations.

What To Do If You Have An Amazing Meditation or a Poor Meditation:
Let go of it. Honestly. Sometimes you will have great meditations and be very peaceful, some days you won't feel like you have any peace. Let go of them both because if you get really attached to the blissful states you will also get attached to the unpleasant states when they come along – when the mind is really busy.

Meditation is the backbone of so many spiritual traditions which have been around for thousands of years and are still here: like Hinduism, Buddhism, Taoism, even certain traditions of Christianity. What is being suggested is that maybe they are onto something – maybe meditation is very powerful – I believe it is life changing and if I can inspire you to pick up one thing from this book and one thing only I would recommend meditation.

When I started meditation I was emotionally shut down, drinking and taking drugs regularly, working very hard and was very miserable. Yes, it took many years as you will find in this book and meditation was not the only practise I did, but since that time there have been amazing shifts in my life. This is the power of meditation; it changes lives. I really recommend you try it. Try it now.

I first started to get interested in spirituality when I lived in London. It was 1997 and I was doing a work placement while still at university. I had just broken up for the first time with my French partner and was feeling rather low. My sister was going out with a spiritually minded man and had lots of spiritual books. So she lent me one. It was called Dance With Life by Susan Jeffers.

I was rather cynical about spirituality and religion until that point due to my upbringing. So I hadn't glanced at religion or spirituality since my school days. But somehow the first book really touched me. By practising what the author was saying started to make me feel better. I started to read other books by Deepak Chopra, The Dalai Lama, Thich Naht Hanh, and many others. Their words really sang to my heart.

One day I was out socialising in London with my work colleagues when I was a salesman. I was just about to leave the pub and I had in my hand a copy of Louise Hay's The Power is Within You. My work colleague asked me what I was reading so I told her. Her jaw dropped, her eyes widened and a look of shock spread across her face. She didn't ask me to repeat the name and I don't think she spoke to me again... Salespeople didn't read things like that!

I learned how to meditate as you heard earlier and realised to myself that meditation itself was simple – the more challenging thing was keeping my mind still. Again it was a few years later in the monastery when I realised that my job was not to keep my mind still, my job was just to sit on that meditation cushion and be with whatever came up. And if that was a really busy mind then so be it!

My connection to spirituality in London helped me immensely. When I first started meditating I found that I would have more perspective on things, for example, when I dropped a carton of milk in my kitchen, I cleaned it up straight away rather than getting angry at myself. This was new for me. Suddenly there was a little distance between my thoughts and my actions. Situations I was making a mess of before suddenly seemed to sort themselves out.

My work life flowed better and for a time I felt happier within myself. I wasn't able to maintain the happy states for long but I kept my meditation practise going. My mind would be all over the place in the morning before I began my commute on London Underground, although not realising that this was okay in meditation.

I also started to get clarity about my life. I started to realise that I didn't want to work in London any more. I had some huge decisions to make and my new found practice and spirituality helped to give me the strength to make them.

I think that the main difference I found in London from being a reasonably heavy drinker and drug taker to starting a spiritual practice was having clarity. I had always felt the need to drink or take drugs because I felt uncomfortable in myself. I didn't enjoy socialising and generally felt that I never had anything of interest to talk to people about. So I drank. And when I drank my tongue loosened or my anger would surface. It hadn't always been pretty. But by meditating on a daily basis I started to see that London wasn't the life for me.

One day my partner and I were walking on Hampstead Heath. We reached the top of Parliament Hill which overlooks London. I remember thinking to myself, "Gosh, there are buildings everywhere – as far as the eye can see. I have to get out of here!" My partner piped up, "Wow, isn't it beautiful!" I knew at this point that we were moving on different paths. I explained how I felt about living in London and in her compassion she said that she would be willing to live on the edge of London in somewhere rural and commute in.

I had definitely opened a door with this meditation practise and saw that there was another way. Indeed things were about to change…

Recap on Using Spirituality To Overcome Stress

Spirituality can really help to overcome stress by helping you to gain perspective in your life. When things seem to get out of control then you can call on this part of yourself to pull yourself through.

- **Investigate The Spirituality That You Are Interested In** – what really interests you – maybe it's meditation or Buddhism or God. Maybe it's connecting to nature and being outside. Connect to your heart and you will find your inner passion and your inner strength to cope with any situation.

- **Living an Upright and Upstanding Life** – do unto others as you would wish them to do unto you. And do unto yourself as you would wish others to treat you.

- **Refrain From Killing Living Things** – becoming aware that all living beings are sacred takes a huge weight off the conscience.

- **Being Gentle and Kind With Your Words** – your words can be like daggers or like blossom petals. Be gentle with your words.

- **Be Compassionate** – see that most people are trying their best but do not always succeed. Open your heart to see that others suffer just as you do and that you don't need to add to their suffering.

- **Being Gentle and Kind With Your Actions** – how generous do you think you can be? How much love and caring can you put into what you do? And this can be towards others just as much as towards yourself.

- **Don't Judge Yourself or Judge Others (Learning to Receive Yourself Now).** (Just as I am writing this I have received a phone call from a family member who was upset at having problems with the internet). We can judge ourselves so much and give ourselves such a hard time when we aren't able to do something. Learn to receive yourself as the beautiful and amazing being that you are.

- **Meditation** is like exercise for your mind. Regular practise will bring great benefits to your whole life.

Chapter Three – Questions

1. What could you change in your life to make you a more honest person (and therefore having less stress)? What do you do that you always justify but know that it is wrong?

2. What are words that you would like to hear from others about yourself? Use these words and phrases to support and lift the people who are around you. By doing this you will hear these words coming from others back to you…

3. Name 10 things you would love to do this week for yourself. Do at least one of them.

4. Where do you judge yourself unfairly and give yourself a hard time? Can you forgive yourself enough to let go of it now?

5. How do you meditate?

CHAPTER 4
How To Reduce Stress At Work

A large proportion of your life is spent working. You spend 5 or maybe six days a week at work so therefore if you are stressed at work this is going to affect the rest of your life.

In fact for most people work is most of their life. So if you are not managing your stress levels while at work or if work is the cause of your stress then your life is generally going to be a stressful life.

On leaving university my partner was also working in banking so I decided that I would enter that field again. I felt that I had the experience to work in banking but the banks felt different. I left university with a 2:2 level degree which was perceived not good enough to get an interview.

After a few months of looking for work in banking I started to look into other areas. I decided that I would have to try sales out. This wasn't my idea of fun but I was lost in the misconception that I had to earn good money and it didn't matter what I did (a bit like my father really).

I eventually got a job working for a financial publishing company doing telesales. Years later I was talking to a used car salesman and told him that I had done telesales. When I mentioned that I had done over a year as a telesalesman he was amazed and said that I had great endurance as telesales was one of the hardest jobs to do.

And indeed it was.

For the first 2 months on the job I received no commission. I had the job of setting up a new arm of the business: no recent database, no leads, just a list of names from a list company most of which were wrong.

So I started calling. My target was to make 50 phone calls a day. I didn't manage to make all the calls and with my colleagues we used to cheat by fixing the system. I probably made between 30 – 40 calls a day.

I found that I had to psyche myself up in order to make calls. I had to sit on the edge of my seat and breathe really deeply. I also started to learn a system for dealing with the different scenarios which came up – no, I am not interested for example.

A lot of my colleagues used the aggressive technique of calling, hassling people even if they weren't interested. They made lots of sales but they also made lots of enemies. I started to do a new approach. I realised from doing door to door sales as a teenager that people's favourite subject was themselves. So I stopped trying to sell and I started to get interested in who I was talking to. I rarely talked about the product and talked more about what the individuals were up to – football, holidays, or weekends. It made it more it more interesting for both parties.

If people said they didn't want me to call again then I wouldn't, but that was very rare. When people were rude to me, I challenged them. I pointed out that I was doing a job and I was human just like them. To receive abuse wasn't very pleasant I pointed out and they seemed to respect this. Looking back, seeing how angry I was, and this is what I was giving off, it is no surprise that people rarely messed me around.

I found the job really challenging. I had always been the silent type so for me to suddenly have to speak to people on a constant basis was very difficult. I learned how to do it but the truth was that I really didn't like what I was doing.

But there were plus sides. Due to the fact I was starting to build relationships with my clients after a few months I started to make commissions. And these commissions grew and grew. One month I remember making £50,000 worth of sales which earned me around £4,000 in commission. This wasn't huge for the City but my company also paid me a regular salary as well. The 2 combined meant that I was earning well.

What I started to notice in the City was that although I was earning good money, living in an expensive part of London with a lovely partner, inside I felt totally unfulfilled. As I looked around me at my colleagues, friends and other City workers

I saw the same thing: they weren't really enjoying themselves – a glance around London Underground in the morning confirmed that! I knew there had to be something more.

I started to look for ways to remedy this and enrolled as a volunteer for an alcohol and prevention services mentoring scheme. I was trained up as a mentor and would then meet regularly with recovering alcoholics giving them advice and support with different areas of their lives: listening, careers advice…

One day I was helping one of the "mentees" with his CV. He was German and couldn't understand why I was helping him. It didn't compute with him. I thought about it and mentioned that I grew up with a father who drank a lot and felt that there was something I could give back by doing this. He was very touched by this and felt more able to relate to me. I sensed a shift in him - whether it was seeing the other side of alcohol, I don't know but somehow a big change happened, in him and in me.

I think I realised at this point how much more satisfied I felt by giving to others, and being of service than I ever did earning lots of money. The money seemed to temporarily satisfy my ego but giving without expectation of return satisfied my heart.

So in this chapter we look at what ways you can help to relieve stress at work. There are many options to overcoming issues at work and many solutions.

25. Taking Regular Breaks

Taking regular breaks is really important during the day. When you are working in the office or at home it can be very easy to be drawn into working non stop.

And this goes for when you are passionate about something as well. Sometimes we can get drawn into doing things and lose track of time. If you are breathing deeply, relaxed and focussed this can be okay as you will feel energized but generally this is not the case.

Generally when you get involved in an activity, be that work or play, you can get sucked into it.

What I have found to work best for myself both in an office environment and a work-from-home situation is to take regular breaks. When I worked in a corporate office I always took a 15 minute break every 2 hours. This meant that I took a break around 10 am and then again at 3pm. This helped to break up the day and the tension in my body.

I took these breaks on top of my hour lunch break.

Now you might say, but I can't take those breaks. Have you asked? I worked out that my colleagues used to go out and have a cigarette at least 3 or 4 times in a day so I felt that it was only right that I went for a break as well. I spoke with my managers and they were always okay with it. At the time, in 2006, the Health & Safety Guidelines in the UK advised that desk-bound workers should have a break every 2 hours.

The benefits of taking regular breaks are as follows:

- Helps to clear the mind
- Helps to relax the body and release tension
- Helps to focus the mind – you might have been lost on one project when it wasn't the thing that you needed to be doing – the break will help you to see your work with new eyes.
- Keeps your stress levels down
- It is said that the mind can only concentrate properly for an hour without needing a break yet many people work for 3 or 4 hours straight without a break
- Helps you to let go of work at the end of the day – your mind will be clearer because you have taken regular breaks.

Now that I am working for myself, I take a break every hour for 15 minutes. I go outside do qigong, tai chi, yoga, exercise, and breathing techniques.

It helps to give me clarity and to refocus my mind on what is important.

26. Write a Daily Schedule

By writing out and then following a daily schedule can be very helpful in keeping focus and can increase productivity greatly. The below exercise will lead you through the process but in essence at the beginning of each day you write out a schedule of tasks you need completing and then you work through them one by one. You take regular breaks, which incorporates the previous point, and you enjoy doing each task. Remember the path is the destination so find some aspect which is enjoyable.

Writing out a list at the beginning of the day or even the night before helps you to see what needs doing (research has shown that by doing it the night before the unconscious mind can then go about pulling the internal resources together to get the work done while you sleep). Then if you get distracted during the day through Facebook or emails, or a colleague when you work in an office, you can then come back to what you were doing with ease. It is okay to get distracted from time to time, and yet we in the West seem to distract ourselves a lot of the time and are not so productive – news websites, sport, email, forums, ebay and so on. I remember when I was working in an office at the advent of Facebook realising that my colleagues were spending literally half their day on Facebook. I myself used to get distracted by the BBC Sports pages again and again.

Writing a daily schedule out, and being flexible with it helps you to increase wellness immensely. There is no longer the stress that "I've got nothing done," or an underlying feeling that you are wasting your time. You feel focused and by the end of the day you feel you have achieved a lot and will feel really good in yourself. Personally I have found that having a schedule helps to keep me focused. And by writing down what needs to be done before I start working I then know what needs to be done first.

When I don't do this I find that I end up working on things which are not only not important but also a waste of time – reading my emails, following the links on the emails and getting lost in someone else's website for hours at a time.

Work out when you are most productive and do the most important things or the things you have been putting off the most first. I personally am most productive in the morning first thing so this is my time for writing – I write on my books for an hour.

From then on I focus on the other things on my list starting with most important first.

The things that I have found most distracting are emails, getting lost on news or sports websites, or following product offers. Don't get drawn in and you will not only stay more focussed, get more done but also feel good about it.

The following exercise will help you to do just that:

EXERCISE 17

Taking Charge of Your Work Day

You have arrived at work or you are sat at your desk at home. Before you turn the computer on get out a piece of paper or better yet purchase a hard backed A4 notebook and use that.

Step One: Write down all the things that you need to do – reply to emails, call clients, write article, post new content, write new proposal etc.

Step Two: Write down next to your list the order of priority listing 1 next to the most important – or the thing you have been putting off, 2 for the next important, 3 for the next etc.

Step Three: Write down a schedule for the day in one hourly segments e.g.

9.30- 10.30	Write my book
10.45 - 11.45	Write new content for website
12.00 - 1pm	Call client X
1-2pm	Lunch
2-3pm	Do administration and accounts
3.15 - 4.15pm	Create brochure for new workshop
4.30 - 5.30pm	Check emails and reply to correspondence and finish off any tasks not finished.

Step Four: Follow through with schedule. Sometimes you won't have finished in an hour – if this happens a few days running then extend the time spent so you fill another hour e.g. you write new content for 12-1pm as well.

But even if you haven't finished something in the hour, move on to the next thing. This helps you to keep concentration because the mind can switch off if it is doing the same thing for hours at a time.

I personally only write for an hour at a time because I find that I am freshest and the words flow for that time. I can write solidly without taking my fingers off the keyboard. But as soon as I have been writing for more than an hour I start to switch off and I don't enjoy writing as much.

Step Five: Notice when your peak times are. For most people I recommend doing the thing that is most important during your peak time. Now for me that is in the morning, but not for everyone. I know people who can't function before 12 midday. Their best time is just after midnight!

Now that's fine to have different body clocks but it is learning to use this effectively. Obviously, if you need to call business people then just after midnight is not ideal unless you are in the UK and they are based in Australia. By learning to use this effectively you do the most important thing when you are feeling the most energized.

One thing I recommend to people is not to look at emails first thing. This is a distraction – and can start your day off being completely distracted and stay distracted and off kilter all day.

Step Six: Set your alarm for the breaks. As soon as the alarm goes stop what you are doing and put the computer on standby. By putting the computer on standby you do not have to close any programs.

A lot of people don't have breaks because they feel they have to finish something before they can have a break. And as one thing leads to another they never have a break.

So by doing this method you don't need to have finished anything. Turn the computer off and come back 15 minutes later.

What I find by doing this is that sometimes I have got lost in my email or looking at something which is not adding value to my life. By putting the breaks in it means that you have clarity when you come back from the break and see things with more clarity. You can then adjust and refocus yourself.

Step Seven: Things you haven't done need to be moved to the list on the next day. What you will find is that you will put off the things that need doing the most. Sometimes I will go back over my daily task lists and see that I haven't done the same thing day after day. I then move this to the first item and do it first.

The reason I haven't done that item is usually because of fear. It feels so much better doing the things that are easy. But actually by not doing something continually puts that thought in the back of your head - tapping away on your subconscious, "I should be doing this... I should have done it... I am no good... Why can't I get anything done... I am not trustworthy because I never follow through with anything."

So make sure you carry the things not done onto the next day's list.

The above exercise is invaluable. Not only will you become more productive but you will also get more focused in your life. The things you have been putting off will start to be crossed off your list one by one and suddenly you will find yourself with free time.

27. Learn To Delegate

If you've got too much work on then ask others to help out. You'll be surprised how others will react. We always presume no one wants to help but sometimes people are only too willing to help. It depends how you ask.

By not telling your managers and colleagues that you have too much on, you add to your stress levels.

But it is important that you do it in a proactive way. Ask your managers or colleagues to help rather than talking behind their backs that the work levels are ridiculous. This is likely to get back to them so that by the time that you do ask they will have already formulated a response and it is likely to be negative.

Ask yourself how it makes you feel when people talk behind your back and you will know what they will be feeling.

By talking behind people's backs you add to your stress levels – use this energy to change the stressful situation you are in and get help! In doing this you bring about your own empowerment. Ask to speak to your manager and tell them where you are at e.g. "I am struggling to get all this work done. Are there any solutions?" Managers can be in the dark sometimes with their employees and have to guess what is going on. By being up front will always be a breath of fresh air.

The above example is the exact way I approached my managers when working post-monastery. I had just started a new job and was finding it pretty challenging. I told my managers and we had a really productive meeting where they took time to go over what was coming up and to see if they could help. It did certainly help.

If you are working for yourself then there are ways you can delegate or outsource as well. There are many outsourcing companies from taking phone calls, to building websites, to taking care of administration. It is the type of thing we put off for a long time but when we do outsource we are so grateful for the extra time. Where are the areas you can delegate or outsource to others?

28. Get Out Of The Office For Lunch

Try not to sit at your desk for lunch. By sitting at your desk for lunch means that you don't get a proper break and you don't get any fresh air. And if you eat food at your desk while working this does not help digestion – the more relaxed and calm you are while eating the more benefit you get out of your food.

If you are stressed while you eat then this stress goes straight to the stomach. Get out for a break, a walk, a sit in the park, listen to music, meet with a friend. By breathing in fresh air or just breathing in a relaxed and calm way while eating helps digestion and the amount of energy you get out of your food.

If you are not digesting your food you are not going to be getting a lot of the nutrition from your food – it will pass straight through your gut.

And also by not having a break, and by being at your desk all day you only add more stress to your life. I personally used to find that I stopped thinking straight if I had been in the office all day without a break. I stopped thinking clearly and therefore made bad choices in my work and later on in my life.

When you don't take care of yourself during the day this rubs off into other areas of your life – you feel really tired by the end of the day and then make poor decisions – staying up all night, saying unpleasant things, not taking care of your body...

By having regular breaks and getting out of the office for lunch means that you feel clearer after lunch. And by the end of the day because you have eaten well, in a relaxed manner and you have taken regular breaks you feel clearer and therefore your work and personal life really benefit from it.

The following is a really lovely exercise you can do while on your lunch break.

EXERCISE 18

Feeling Body Sensations

1. This exercise can be done either sat done or while walking. It is best to be done alone, or if others want to practise with you then great. What is important is that you are silent for at least 5 minutes. It is easier to be sat down as you can close your eyes.

2. Start to become aware of the sensations of your body. Start at your left toes and slowly move up the left leg to the left buttock, feeling the sensation of your legs touching your clothing or the ground. Do they feel warm, cold, is there any discomfort or deep relaxation? Then move to the right toes and move up the right leg with your attention.

3. Use your attention to start flowing up your back, then up your front torso. Then move to your left shoulder taking your attention then down your left arm to your hand. Feel the sensations of your body. If your mind gets distracted with gentleness and kindness move back to the place you last remember focusing on.

4. Move your attention to your right shoulder and then down your right arm to your right hand. Then finally move your attention up your neck into your head and face. How do the muscles feel?

5. Now bring your awareness to your whole body from the tips of your toes to the top of your head. And hold that awareness.

6. The more you practise this exercise the more present you will feel throughout the day. This will mean that you are less likely to get pulled into stressful situations or get distracted by others. You will learn a great sense of peace and joy. This can also form part of your meditation practise.

This is a really powerful exercise and one which when practised regularly on your lunch breaks will bring you a great sense of refreshment. A sense of clarity will return to you and you will find yourself able to focus more clearly and concisely. Tasks which you were struggling on before lunch will fall into place.

It is so important for us as humans to be at our optimum when doing anything. We so often choose to feel negative without making any effort to change this. What unfolds is more negative situations to match where we are at. It is paramount that we do the practices, like the one above, to get us into as good a feeling space as possible. Why? Life is meant to be joyful, life is meant to be fun, life is meant to be abundant and life affirming. And when we are not feeling that way it is up to us, nobody else, to change how we are feeling.

And how do we do that you ask? By following the exercises and ideas from this book, is one way. But there are so many other ways of getting to the same destination. You've just got to start walking the path. When you don't feel so good. Stop. Yes, stop. Take a break and do what you can to lift yourself, change how you are feeling. Take any of the tools from this book and practice them. Do them as often and as regularly as you can. Through regular practise it starts to become second nature, just as you don't think to brush your teeth, you just do it. So when you start to feel negative or wobbly you just breath deeply or you focus on the sensations of your body.

You are an amazing being. You have such potential within. And with the breath and with the practise you will start to tap into this. You can feel this now as you read this. You know you have this potential. It is there and like a diamond in the rough. You are starting to uncover your inner diamond in this very moment. Well done. Well done!

29. Learning From The Negative And Critical People In The Office.

This type of person can create stress in your life. Being around really negative or critical people can for some be really draining. Indeed, you won't feel energised by them and they seem to sap your energy. They can put you down and make you feel bad about yourself. It is not pleasant to work in an office with this type of situation.

The interesting thing about negative colleagues is that, as with most things I will teach in this book, they are great teachers and show you where you are at.

Indeed, what you will find as you practise the exercises in this book is that you will no longer be drawn to being around the negative people. Why? Well, when you challenge your own negativity and no longer put up with it from yourself, therefore you no longer put up with it from others – you will just find that you are not in the same room. If you are then it is important to work out why these people are attracted to you. Why does it bother you? What are they reflecting about you? Do your colleagues talk to you like your internal critic talks to you?

It works as a 2 way thing. The negative person is showing you where you are at. The negative person feels comfortable with you if you are always with them. Likewise if you are always around positive and uplifting people then they are showing you where you are at.

And as we practise more with tools like compassion we will see that this person is really hurting just as we were when we gossiped or were nasty. Your heart opens and through this you start to heal yourself and those around you. You no longer see them as bad but see them as wonderful teachers.

30. Learn To Focus On One Task At A Time

Learning to focus on one task at a time is a novel idea in a multitasking world. We are told that to do many things at once is a great idea. We are told that to do many things at one time is great. And on one level it is in certain situation, or for a certain period of time. But to do this on a continual basis can drain you of energy. Multitasking is a bit like having your foot pressed against the accelerator – really useful to pull away from another car in a dangerous situation but you wouldn't want to drive like that all the time.

In my own corporate experience I found that focusing on one task at a time was very powerful. Especially when I have had lots of work on I have found this technique wonderful in coping with stress.

EXERCISE 19

One Task At A Time

1. Clear your desk and place all outstanding things in one pile. This means that your desk has no paperwork on it apart from the one pile in the corner of your desk. Close all programs on your computer and leave open the one program that you need e.g. Microsoft Word or Excel, or Quickbooks.

2. You then pull one item or chore at a time from your pile and then focus on that, and solely that. If you are working on the computer and are answering emails stick to the task. There will be many easy ways to get distracted – by following links or looking at the news. But for at least an hour at a time (have a break after an hour) keep your focus.

3. If you are working in an office environment and someone comes to give you more work, then ask them to leave it in the pile.

4. If someone needs your attention, ask them how urgent it is – can it wait 30 minutes or an hour? If not deal with it and then come back to where you were. If it can wait, make a note somewhere to go and speak to that individual when you have finished. Learn to be firm.

This is a technique I used in a big American corporation I was working in after my monastic days. I found that it reduced my stress greatly as I was very present doing one thing and one thing only. I heard one of the senior managers saying a very similar thing when he was working on something very important – "please come back in 30 minutes". By doing this technique you do the same amount of work (if not more) but it is a lot less stressful (try it – it certainly works for me).

You can add this element to the Taking Charge of Your Work Day Exercise. It means that you look at what you have to do before you start your day and then you focus on that and only that – it means that you don't go opening emails as you receive them – you deal with emails or phone calls at a certain time in the day.

I once read a story from a successful online businessman who had gone off to do some training with one of his mentors.

They had planned to have 4 hours training together but when they were just about to start the secretary came into the office. She started to say that there was an urgent call from the mentor's landlord – there was a problem with the property and he needed to call urgently. She then went on to say that his wife called and said he needed to call back. She continued and said that the photocopier was not working and she had some urgent things to print up.

The mentor looked at her and asked that she backed herself up, went out of the room and didn't disturb them for the next 4 hours.

Four hours went by and the two people managed to get much work done and many things completed. When they came out of the office they found out that the landlord had called back to say that the problem was solved, the photocopier was now fixed and that the wife called to say her problem was resolved as well.

This story just shows that so often we react to situations and we get pulled into them – we open the emails as they arrive, we get distracted when our friend posts about her party last night... What happens is that we get very little work done, because we are always reacting and not working on things which are of most importance. And what happens when we just focus? As in the story, if there are problems more often than not when we stop worrying they just sort themselves out and you get a tremendous amount of work done.

31. Keep Breathing

It's very easy to forget to breathe when you are working or in the office. When you get focused on something breathing can be the first thing that you forget to do. So where possible you can over exaggerate breathing. Breathe slowly and deeply, and relax the shoulders and body.

If you can breathe as much as possible during the day you will find that you have more focus, more calm and more clarity around decisions than you ever thought possible.

Breathing through the nose where possible is another great way of deepening the sense of relaxation. When we breathe through the nose we filter up to 50% more oxygen into the blood than when we breathe through the mouth. The nasal passageways are smaller and this restriction as we breathe out means that the lungs are able to extract more oxygen.

Try this now as you are reading this. Breathe through the nose slowly in then out. And how do you feel? Does it relax you, focus your mind and bring a sense of peace?

Another reason for breathing through the nose is that the synapses which regulate our breathing are located there. This means that when you breathe through the nose the body and unconscious mind takes care of breathing in a regular pattern. You can get on and do other things and the body will be taking care of breathing for you. When you breathe through the mouth on the other hand you bypass these synapses. Have you have ever noticed yourself snatching for breath every now and then when you are really busy and breathing through your mouth? You will also notice this more profoundly when you have a cold and are not able to breathe through the nose.

There are many other reasons for breathing through the nose from filtering out germs, to warming the air but the point is that it is really beneficial to be breathing through the nose.

Are you still breathing through the nose now? And how does it feel? Excellent – well done... The following exercise will help you to further relax. This exercise can be done in any seated location but was primarily devised for while in an office or sat at a desk.

Every 30 minutes to an hour practise this exercise. You don't have to get up from your desk and you can place your hands on the keyboard or on the mouse so that to the onlooker it looks like you are working. But in fact – you are taking a power relaxation recharge.

EXERCISE 20

Power Relaxation Recharge

Please fully read through this exercise before practising it

1. Get comfortable and sit with your spine straight and your head, neck and shoulders relaxed. Take a deep breath in through the nose focusing on your head and shoulder area. As you breathe out slowly through the nose feel your neck, shoulders and head relaxing.

2. Find a spot at eye level in front of you either on your computer or just in front of you which you can focus on. I used to use the Windows icon on my computer screen.

3. All breathing is done through the nose in this exercise. Focus on your chosen spot and then breathe in and then out slowly. Count 1.

4. Continue to count to 20 while focusing on the spot in front of you while keeping your head, neck and shoulders relaxed.

5. The mind will want to wander and you might find yourself looking at something on the screen or wanting to get distracted and pick up some mental object. Keep the focus – you can do it and you are doing it! Keep bringing your attention back to the present moment and to counting your slow, regenerative breaths.

6. Have a few moments at the end of the exercise when you allow your eyes to drop and you check in where you are at – how do you feel?

32. Remember That It's Just A Job.

We take our jobs very seriously, too seriously sometimes. And this affects our health. Do what you can do to the best of your ability, but be gentle, be kind.

If your job is your passion then you will find that it will really feed you; you feel energized and alive. But even when it really feeds you it is important to have breaks, to have time where you are not doing your passion.

For a lot of people who do work with their passion they can get so embroiled in it, become so addicted to it that their lives around them fall apart – relationships fail, families leave, health deteriorates.

So it is really important as with everything in life to have balance, to have time to be in your passion but then time to rest and recuperate, time to spend with your family. If you don't take this time you will find that your passion will quickly turn into a job, a chore, a pain. Don't let it become that way and structure in regular breaks, and time off .

If it is not your passion then ever more important to be gentle with yourself. I always found in a corporate environment that the person that was toughest with me was not my boss for X company or my colleague from Y, but yes, you guessed, it was me. Often times, you are the greatest critic of you. Not your boss, spouse, children, or colleagues. Although sometimes we can put words in their mouths through our imaginings of what they are saying, but really it is us being critical of ourselves.

Think back to how many times people have criticised us? Probably very few times and yet sometimes we can feel like we are being criticised all the time. And yet this is coming from us.

So what to do about this? Firstly, as we have talked about already do the practises here – the breathing, taking regular breaks, doing the meditation on a daily basis – these practises start to challenge the inner critic. Secondly, do the following exercise. It comes from NLP and I have found it very useful to deal with the critical inner voices.

EXERCISE 21

Dealing With The Inner Critic

Please read through this exercise fully before practising it

1. When you become aware of a critical voice in your head, stop. Notice it. Where do you imagine the voice is?

2. What is it saying? As you hear it saying these words see the voice float out of yourself so that it is about 3 metres from you.

3. Replay the same words so that they are coming from 3 metres away but this time in a funny voice – like Donald Duck, or Mickey Mouse. Keep repeating the phrase in this funny voice and until it no longer bothers you to hear it.

4. Try this out with other phrases you have found annoying or upsetting in the past – keeping the voice 3 metres away and if needs be push it further away and turn the volume down on the voice. Remember to keep the voice ridiculously funny! Use a favourite character from a funny film.

This is a great tool for taking the sting out of the inner critic. You can practise the above tool before the critic appears using examples of times and things that you say to yourself sometimes - "I'm no good, I'm not good enough, I'll never be enough, you're stupid..."

33. You Learn When Things Are Challenging

This is an important thing to remember – that the times when you are feeling challenged are the times when you grow the most. When you are in it, going through the challenge, it doesn't seem like that, but when you look back in hindsight you see that when you were pushed to the edge you had to find an extra something from somewhere. Indeed, you are still here so it means that you survived it and you learnt from it.

The author and teacher Esther Hicks talks about this time being really important for the process of working out what it is that you do want. When it is stressful or things are chaotic these are the times that, as she says, you send out a rocket of desire. So for example it's chaotic at work. You know that you want it to be relaxing or stress-free, or fun, or joyful. So that moment of chaos helps you to clarify what you do want.

The author Michael Losier says that there is a simple question you need to ask yourself when you are feeling challenged or that things are not going the way you want them to go. You ask yourself:

So what do I want?

And in that moment of challenge you clarify, "Oh, I want it to be easy..." And the interesting thing is that sometimes just by making that thought can stretch you so that suddenly even though there is chaos around you, you feel relaxed. Suddenly by making that thought you feel at ease. It is like you are the eye of the storm. It rages around you but everything is stillness within, it doesn't affect you, you are watching on.

For example, your dog is barking all the time – so this becomes I want my dog to become silent.
You have no money – I want money to flow in.
Your work is stressful – I want my work to be enjoyable and fun.

Try it the next time there is a challenging situation and give all your focus to the solution, e.g. I want money to flow in. By doing that you will find that the pathway will open up so that you find yourself very quickly in that place of what you want.

34. Get A Pot Of Nuts To Munch At Your Desk.

Having a healthy snack by your desk helps to keep you energized. It is possible to get so embroiled and lost in your work that you don't take breaks or even lunch breaks. We can work until we start to feel a bit dizzy so we quickly pop down to the local store to pick up a bag of crisps or a bar of chocolate. We go back to work while munching this snack, but we don't feel energized – the sugar and carbs will give us a little hit and fill a little hole but soon we feel sluggish again.

A pot of nuts or a piece of fruit like an apple, banana, bag of dates or figs or apricots release their energy slowly. This type of food helps to keep your mind clearer and your thoughts more focused. Rather than giving you a hit where you are really productive for 30 minutes and then return to sluggish state, you will find you have a balanced amount of energy. As with a lot of these techniques, they become more powerful when they are put together. So you eat your bag of figs, have a break, have a lunch break, have a walk...

Some people find that when they are working hard they eat the first thing they can get their hands on. They are focused on their work so that eating is not important. So the importance of preparation is everything. It is important to stock your larder so that you have fruit and nuts and seeds, available if you are working at home or in your bag and at hands reach if you are working in an office. It is another step into well-being and clarity. Eat healthy, slow energy release food and the mind and body love it. You will get so much more work done.

35. Keep Your Office Space As Tidy As Possible.

By having a tidy desk you help yourself to focus on the task at hand. By having paper everywhere, you will end up going from one thing to the next and not feel like you have got anything done.

Spend 30 minutes every week tidying up, 5 minutes every day putting things in order. You might feel like you are not getting much done but I assure you, little by little your space will become clearer and yes, surprisingly enough so will your mind.

The meditation teacher Ajahn Chah, said that if you want to work out the meditation practise of a monk, or a monastery, don't look at how many hours they spend on the meditation cushion but by how clean their toilets are! What this is saying is that the outer reflects the inner. When you take care of the outer so the inner is cleaned. When you clean the inner, through meditation and breathing, so the outer is cleansed – our relationships improve, we feel happier...

So take a little time to clean your desk. Have you had things sitting on your desk for years that you don't use? Tidy the space every day. Throw things away which you don't use. Clear things to their correct places – dirty cups to a kitchen, and rubbish to a bin.

36. Some Days It Feels Like You Have Got Nothing Done...

There are days like that. You work all day and feel as if you have done nothing. This is life. Some days are like that. Remember that some days are very productive. Life is a balance. So don't get too stressed when you don't feel you've got anything done.

The important thing is that you do whatever you do from a space of joy. This can be a challenge to start off with, but after a period of time, you will find that you're not rushing to finish things, so that you can start to move to the next thing, but to embrace this moment.

A powerful spiritual teaching that we have spoken before about is that:

The Path Is The Destination

We are forever striving for the goal, the destination, the want, the need but it would seem in the West that we have forgotten that life is meant to be fun. Life is amazing when we stop. Life is amazing when we stop striving. Yes, there are days when it feels like you have done nothing, but when you are in your bliss, when you are enthused and passionate, it doesn't matter.

Remember this as you rush through your day. Remember to remember. This moment. The here, the now. For if we struggle to get to a destination, well, the destination is a struggle as well. As we've already discussed in the chapter on finances, so many financially rich people are not wealthy, they are not happy for they are always striving to get to the next goal, and then the next one after that.

Live this moment as if it is the most wonderful moment to be alive. We are blessed, you are blessed. So remember that if you make it your gift to yourself to enjoy this moment then it doesn't matter if you feel like you get lots done or nothing done.

EXERCISE 22

Living This Life As The Most Wonderful Moment Alive

Please read through this exercise fully before experiencing. Please note it will take a little practise before becoming fluent with it.

1. Remember a few amazing times from your life – write them down.

2. Breathe in and picture the first amazing time in front of you so that you are looking up (important that the eyes are looking up). Breathe out and let the image grow in colour, feel the feelings, and hear the sounds around you. Make the image as big as possible.

3. Breathe a total of 3 times while looking, feeling, hearing this first experience.

4. Breathe in for the 4th time and visualise the next amazing time, be that a holiday, a time as a child, a magical memory with family or loved ones, or in nature – the sea, a forest, or a lake. Follow the same steps as in Step 2.

5. Breathe another total of 3 times for this image and then move to the next image.

6. You can add images from your Vision Movie, and you can also change pictures every breath.

This tool is one of the most powerful in this book. Taking an example from my own life, I had been visualising happy times with the children I have worked with – laughing, playing, having fun as my happy memories. What unfolded was amazing. Within a day or two of starting the above practise I kept bumping into amazingly happy and joyful children who would just wave at me in the street or come running over even if I didn't know them. I also bumped into one of my Godchildren twice within a few days even though I hadn't seen him for 3 or 4 months...

This practice is powerful. It really is. What we fill our conscious mind with overflows into the outer world. It does seem to work like magic. So make an effort to do the above exercise as much as possible. Take a 5 minute break once an hour and get into an amazing feeling space.

This is what life is about – feeling good. And this exercise helps us to feel good in this moment. To be present and happy and joyful. To be the path rather than the destination. It is all within us now. The feelings, the joy are all here to be experienced now. And when you do feel this, well, watch the magic start to unfold in your life. So although you might feel like you are not getting anything done – it doesn't matter because life is feeling – yes, feeling amazing...

37. Use Affirmations As To Shift From Negative To Positive

Your mind is a big factor in your well-being. The internal dialogue that you have playing in your head, as we have spoken about before, makes a huge difference in your stress levels. And yet most of the time we are not aware that this voice is playing, or indeed what it is playing.

The first thing to become aware of when you are working is,

How am I feeling?

If you have just done the above exercise then you will be feeling great. If you are not feeling great then start to pay attention to what you are thinking. What is your mind telling you? What are you thinking about?

Looking back to my own experience I found that the below exercise was very powerful. I was working for an American corporation in the UK. I had just changed position from UK Delivery Query Manager to French Customer Services and Supermarket Stock Manager. The change in language although my French was still good, made a big difference when communicating with clients. I couldn't say what I wanted to say.

And then there was the French summer holidays. In France, as with most of Southern Europe, everyone goes on holiday in August. This is great if you are looking after supermarkets in the big cities – stock levels are low and no one's buying. But if you are looking after the smaller supermarkets in the South of France – well, just watch the products fly off the shelves! And then I worked out that instead of it taking me a day to get stock to the supermarkets as was the case with the northern supermarkets it took 2 days and sometimes longer because of bank holidays.

I had only been in the job for about 5 weeks when August arrived and by Jove, I found it rather stressful. I didn't know what I was doing and yes, you guessed it, my supermarkets ran out of my products – whoops.

And yet the powerful teaching was watching my mind. This again is powerful. There was a lot of work on but on top of that my mind was shouting, "There's too much work," "I can't do this," "This is ridiculous!" And those thoughts made life 10 times more stressful. As I carried out the below exercise a weight lifted off my shoulders and although the work level had not changed I felt a million times better.

EXERCISE 23

Catching Your Blurts & Turning Them Around

1. When you are working place a piece of paper and a pen next to your keyboard, laptop or work surface (a pen and piece of paper is fine as well).

2. When you start to feel stressed, anxious, or in a not feeling good place become aware of what your inner dialogue (your blurts) is saying to you. e.g. There's too much work, I can't cope with this, I'm so slow.

3. Later on when you are having a break or maybe at the same time that you write down the blurts (be aware when you are not feeling as good, that it is not as easy to find any alternatives) take hold of your list.

4. Go through your list and find the positives for your blurts e.g.:
    - There's too much work – There's just the right amount of work for me.
    - I can't cope with this – I am coping with this
    - I'm so slow – I work at exactly the right pace

5. Leave this list next to your desk or worksurface for at least a week. When things get stressful and the inner dialogue starts up look at the list and change the words in your head. Repeat them over and over again in your head. "I am coping with this," or whatever words you have come up with.

6. After that the first week, keep the list close at hand and pull it out whenever you hear the inner dialogue going again.

Like all these exercises, this again is powerful. These exact blurts were the ones which I wrote down on my piece of paper while working that summer (I still have my piece of paper hidden in one of my files...). These were the negative voices making a stressful situation a lot harder. But by changing them around took a huge sting out of the stress I was feeling. I could feel my shoulders relaxing as I said the words "I am coping" in my head. The work situation hadn't changed but I felt so much more at ease. So what if they didn't have any nappies in Biarritz! They would arrive when I could get them there.

And on the opposite swing you can use this exercise to start to use your mind to create great joy. Repeating the words, "I am doing an amazing job" or "This project's going to be amazing" while feeling great about it gives extra impetus to finishing and doing a project well. Try it out and see.

38. Doing The Job You Love

For most people this idea of doing the job you love can seem like a very foreign idea.

"Doing something I love? But I have to make money…"

"That's ridiculous! Whatever I love will become the thing that I really hate!"

"I don't know what I love!"

"Doing what you love is just for hobbies…"

Does this sound familiar? Does this sound like something you feel about your own life and your own job?

The key with doing what you love is to start now. We have spoken several times about the present moment and about how the path is important not the destination. Well, the same applies here. If you want to be doing a job you love you have to start loving the job you are doing now.

"But it's horrible, the people are terrible, the pay is poor..."

Your task is to start to get into a better feeling space. So many of the exercises in this book will help you to do this, choose one. Exercise 22: *Living This Life As The Most Wonderful Moment Alive*, will help you to get into a better feeling space now. That is step one. Do all you can do to start to feel better in this moment.

Step 2 is to start to feel grateful for what you do have in your work at the moment. Follow through Exercise 4 on Gratitude and find some things to be grateful for within your job – I get paid, I enjoy the work, there is a person there who is really kind and inspiring, it gets me out of the house, I get to work outside... Whatever you can find draw on those. Write them down so that you can come back to them when you are not feeling so good about your job.

Step 3 is to start to look and enquire into what it is you do want. Yes, I am not saying that you have to stay in your "unpleasant" job for the rest of your life. What I am saying is that until you start to change how you feel about your work life **now** you will probably pull the same things into your new job. Until we deal with our stuff we just carry it around with us like baggage. And this can be applied to any area of your life. You move to a new company which to start off with is great, but gradually you start to hang your baggage on the coat hooks of the new organisation – the complaining mind, the workaholic tendencies. And this new organisation becomes very similar to the one you just left.

So your job now in this moment is to appreciate what you do have, to get into a better feeling space in this moment – not when you get to the new job. The new job is coming just as quickly as you feel better now. So what do you want to do? The following exercise will help you to clarify what you do want and is based on the author Michael Losier again. This exercise helps to clarify what you want by looking at what you don't want. Many people have no idea where to start in terms of what they want but have many dislikes. This exercise helps you to find clarity from these dislikes.

EXERCISE 24

Clarity Through Contrast

1. The following exercise will take about 10-20 minutes. Set aside this time when you won't be disturbed.

2. Get a piece of paper (best not to use your journal for the first part as we will be cutting the paper up) and draw a line down the middle so you have 2 columns - write down at the top of the page "My Ideal Job/ Career". On top of the left column write "The Contrast – What I Don't Want" and in the right hand column write, "The Clarity – What I Do Want".

3. Start to list on the left hand side all the things you don't like about your present job or situation. Write down all the things that annoy and irritate you or make you angry about your current job or situation. For example, I don't like having no money, I hate the negative people in the office, I feel so bored at work, being sat at a desk, feeling really stressed.

4. Make as many entries on the left hand side as possible. Leave the right hand side blank for the time being.

5. Now start to go through the list on the left one by one and change the negative to positive asking the question so what do I want?. So taking the examples in step 3 we change:
   - I don't like having no money – I have lots of money, I am in the process of attracting abundance to me, money flows to me;
   - I hate the people in the office – I work with amazing people who really lift and feed me, I am in the process of attracting really positive people to work with;
   - I feel so bored at work – I want to be stimulated by my work, I do work which I love, or I am in the process of attracting work that I am passionate about;
   - being sat at a desk – working outside, doing physical work
   - feeling really stressed at work – feeling really calm and relaxed at work.

6. You now have a list of all the things you want in a job. If you think of other positives then list them in the right hand side. Now cut the page in half and bin or burn the left hand side. You could also just copy the right hand side column into your journal.

7. Stick the list up near to your desk if you work at home or somewhere prominent in your home where you can glance at it every day if you work in an office. You now have a really clear vision of what your ideal job will be!

8. You can also use this list to add images to your Vision Movie from Exercise 11.

Well done – you now know what you want from your job. You now know what you do want to be doing for a career. One of the most important things is to get down on paper what you want. Many times we go through long periods of time when we don't know what we want – and yet we're not really enjoying what we are doing. By doing the exercise above you have just made huge leaps in your life.

There is an analogy about a ship setting out to sea. If you were to set sail from a port but you have no destination, or bearings on which to set your course you would likely not even get out of the port. If on the other hand you had a destination and you had the resources, the fuel, and the crew then there would be a high probability that you would arrive at your destination.

This analogy ties in with working out what you do want in life, what you do want in a career. Until you work out the destination then you are likely to be stuck in port for a long time. Take the time to do the above exercise and place it somewhere you can look at it and feel the wonderful sensations of knowing the job, the career, your desires are on their way. Once you have done the exercise – you have set sail – congratulations!

When you get lost, distracted, bored, keep coming back to your list – your bearings. And you will get there.

But it is also about remembering to look out of the ship's windows, to enjoy the journey, for as you have learned in the past lessons in this book the path, the journey is the most important part. Enjoy life now.

39. What Is It That You Love?

This point ties in perfectly with the above suggestion about getting clarity about what you do want. This point helps you to really start to take care of the journey – what do you love in life? How can I make this life more fulfilling so the journey becomes one of deep pleasure and excitement.

Well, the following exercise will help you to gain deeper knowledge into what you do want.

EXERCISE 25

Finding Your Passion

Step One: Get out your journal and try to answer as honestly as possible the following questions?

1. In all my life, from my earliest memories, what did I love doing? What was my passion in life? (A lot of us abandon our passions through pressure from family or peers.)
2. What were the activities that sparked me? What were the activities that made me feel alive?
3. What were the happiest times in my life? And why were they so happy?
4. When did I feel most fulfilled?

Once you have answered all these questions – spend at least 5 – 10 minutes on each question – look through your answers. Can you feel that spark of energy or passion running through your body for anything on your list? Write next to each thing you have on your list a number from one to ten (10 for most passionate to 1 for little passion).

Step Two: Pick one of the activities on your list which is ranked highest. If you don't have anything on the list above 7, trawl deeper, think about anything you would love to do in your life. Think of something that you have always been drawn to but for financial reasons, time constraints, or family commitments have not done.

Step Three: Once you have one highly placed item start to do some research on it. Google it, see if there are any classes around, buy a book on it, talk to people about it. For example if you have always wanted to work with horses, start to immerse yourself in horses. Go and volunteer at the local horse stables, buy some books about horses, go to a gymkhana etc....

By doing this you firstly start to see if this is indeed your passion, and secondly you start to meet people who have like-minded interests. You will start to make friends who share your passion and you will find yourself immersed in a group of people who have something in common with.

40. How To Earn A Living From Your Passion

Well, it is possible as you can see. And once you do start to go to groups and meet people who have similar interests you will start to notice that there are some who indeed make a living from their passion.

So why can't you? What's stopping you?

Primarily the thing that stops you from doing what you love is fear. Yes, fear of the unknown and fear of seeming a failure among others.

We are so frightened of moving out of our comfortable spaces. So what happens? We stay stuck, prepared to live a half life doing what we don't enjoy doing, being bored out of our brains because of fear.

Fear is a powerful emotion, just like anger, but as I was always taught by my teacher, there is nothing wrong with the feeling of fear or anger. But what happens is that we don't acknowledge it or we push it under the carpet or we make rash decisions because of it.

One of the primary reasons for not doing what you love is fear of not having enough money. How will I survive if I'm doing something I love? How will I get by?

We have these strange notions inside of ourselves saying that these statements are true. Yet we have never tried to see any other way. We have never tried it out.
In my own life firstly I never knew what it was that I loved. I had no idea. I had been trained not to really think about what my passions were, more what other people's passions were. What did my parents want? What was expected of me?

So at the age of 23, as you have heard before, after completing my education and studying for 4 years at university, I found myself working in the City in London doing telesales.

Why did I take a job in telesales? Fear… fear of not getting a job, for I had been looking for a while and not found anything. I also took it because I felt that money and success were a way to happiness… But sadly I was not doing what I loved. Sure, I learned a lot. I learned patience, I learned what it felt like not to fit in, I learned a whole lot about stress and I learned what it felt like to get paralysed into a life which was draining me.

I learned how it felt to be locked into a spiral of work and recovery, for there was no time or energy for anything else. But how did I get out of this situation? I think the key was seeing that I was trying to live someone else's life. I was trying to live the way of the Everyman, not the way of me.

I was trying to conform…

I was trying to fit in…

But I didn't fit in and this was painful. Does this sound familiar?

I realised that I needed to change, change the way I looked at life and I needed to step into a huge great gaping place of fear.

I took the step…

And I wouldn't be here talking to you if I hadn't taken it. It was very frightening and people did hurt in the short term because of the decisions I made but in the long term everyone gained.

Everyone got what they needed. People around me benefited greatly in the long run – my company got people in who were more passionate about work than I.

So how do you start to make a living from your passion? The first step is to start stepping into your fear:

EXERCISE 26

Stepping into Your Fear:

Step One: Get your journal out. Write down a list of things which you are frightened of doing. Maybe it is to write a book, perform in front of other people, ask the person you love out on a date, speak your truth about a situation to your family or friends… Learning to sing, learning to swim, swimming in the middle of the ocean, rock-climbing, skydiving, fear of heights, fear of spiders, fear of your mother-in-law, fear of doing what you love…

The list needs to be extensive so spend about 20 to 30 minutes on it.

Step Two: Next to each point write down from 1 to 10 how much each of these things frightens you: 1 being not very much and 10 being paralysis.

Step Three: Choose one of the lower numbered items on the list: those that don't frighten you much. Go out and challenge yourself with that fear. For example, a few years ago I realised that I was frightened of heights. I used to love heights as a child but somewhere along the way to becoming an adult I became frightened of them.

So I challenged myself and started to climb trees. The first time I went up the tree I was petrified – full of fear that I would fall and it seemed so high up.

But I did it; I climbed the tree.

And afterwards, wow, did I feel great. I felt wonderful, really alive and proud of myself.
So I started to climb trees regularly and found that not only was I not frightened any more but I loved doing it. It was great.

And what happened was that I became aware that fear wasn't such a bad thing. Fear, I realised, was a thing to be felt and used in order to focus the mind and body but not to completely paralyse.

And the results in my life was that I started to be able to do things that I had always been frightened of – swimming in deep water, performing in public, approaching a woman for a date…

The more you do this exercise the greater the amount of fear you are willing to address. And the result is amazing, you realise that you can do, be or have whatever you want in your life – it is only your fear which is stopping you from asking, from doing and from acting in the face of fear.

"So I say to you: Ask and it will be given to you; seek and you will find; knock and the door will be opened to you"

So the first step to doing the job you love is learning to challenge that fear; the fear of making the calls you need to make, talking to the people you need to speak to.

And the more you do the easier it gets. But it does require regular practice. Step into the fear and watch your life change. How exciting!

I quit my job in telesales at the end of 1999 and went travelling for 6 weeks. Using the money I had saved up I went to Thailand for 3 weeks and then to Australia for 3 weeks. My partner was only able to get 3 weeks off work so she joined me in Australia for the second half of the holiday.

We got back to London in December. It was dark, cold and gloomy. After spending 6 weeks in the sunshine, I found London to be really claustrophobic. I had had a couple of claustrophobic/ panic attacks on the underground and more recently in Australia (sleeping in a VW camper van while heavily under the influence of drugs) and felt this same feeling crawling over me.

I continued to smoke marijuana which exacerbated my claustrophobic feelings. The feelings about being in London that I was trying to suppress kept poking their heads out while I was stoned. I wanted out of London but was now without work so started to look for a new job.

I found work in a sister company of the financial publishing firm I had just quit. I would be working as a journalist and an analyst for syndicated loans. What's a syndicated loan? It's a big loan really – many millions if not billions of dollars or pounds, but in truth I never really understood much about them.

Around this time my life started to fall apart.

The lies about being in London, and doing jobs I didn't like started to catch up with me, and then there was my father.

I received a phone call from my sister at about 1am on Millennium New Years Day. I had just got back from being on Hampstead Heath for the New Year celebrations. We could see the Central London millennium fire works from Parliament Hill so had been up there. I was stoned and paranoid and had found it really hard being around so many other people. I just wanted to crawl up in a hole and hibernate.

"Dad's had pneumonia this Christmas," said my sister, "And it turns out that it is actually lung cancer."

....

How do you reply to that?

How do you reply to that when you're feeling on top of the world? And how do you reply to that when you are paranoid, panicking and really stoned.

"Oh..."

It was a pretty quick come down I have to say. And not that easy to hear.
It was only later on that we realised as a family that it was terminal. My father wouldn't discuss it so we didn't realise for quite a long time.

It was a big shake up. I was already starting to question everything about my life – my career choice, my relationship, my friends, being in London... I didn't feel that I fitted in. Just as my father would tell me in the coming months, that his whole life was an act, so that was how I was starting to feel.

Looking back now, my father's illness was a great awakening for me in my life. I was half dead and had been for many years – I was emotionally shut down – couldn't cry, couldn't feel love or joy in my heart. I was working hard and spending the weekends smoking weed and recovering from my week of work playing on the Playstation till 2 or 3 in the morning. I had no life. I had few interests. Sure, I had started to meditate and get interested in something else and I guess this is what enabled me to make the step into my greatest folly of all.

Recap on How To Reduce Stress At Work

For most of you, it will probably be work which creates the most stress in your life. As most of you will be spending most of your week at work or doing work, dealing with workplace stress is paramount to overcoming your overall stress levels.

So what have we covered in this chapter?

- **By taking regular breaks** while working, you help to process your thoughts. It gives time for both the body and the mind to rest and therefore you have much more clarity after a brief interlude.

- Before starting your day write out what things you need to do. **Write out a schedule** and times you will complete each task. It is very easy to get distracted so this exercise really helps to focus your mind and to help you to be more productive and therefore less stressed

- **By learning to delegate** you help ease the pressure of work around you. If you work for yourself, that might be asking your partner to help or to outsource some part of your job to an outside company.

- **Make sure that you get out of the office for lunch**. By eating at your desk you are not helping your digestion and are therefore not getting as much nourishment out of your food. Getting out of the office also helps you to clear your mind

- Try to **avoid the negative and critical people** in the office as this can add stress to your life.

- By learning to **focus on one task at a time**, especially when you are really busy, you will find that you are not only less stressed but also more focused. And at the end of the day you will find that you have got so much more done.

- When we work most of us forget to breathe. **Keep breathing** and you will be more relaxed and less likely to get stressed.

- Sometimes we forget that our **job is just a job**. Do your best but don't drive yourself into an early grave. Keep breathing and smiling!

- **When things are busy and challenging at work remember that this is the time that you learn the most.** Through personal experience I have learned most of what I teach now. So only through getting it wrong or making mistakes have I truly learned the most. It is not necessarily pleasant but you can turn it around by seeing that you have a wonderful opportunity to learn.

- By **getting a pot of nuts or fresh fruit to eat at your desk** you help to keep your energy levels high.

- **Keep your office space as tidy as possible** and you will feel less stressed. A desk full of papers, or an email box which is overflowing makes it seem that there is more work than there actually is. Clean your desk and email box and you feel like you are dealing with things as they come in rather than fire fighting all the time.

- Some days it will feel like you have got nothing done, don't let yourself worry about it – usually those are the days you have focused on the things that you have been putting off because they take so long! Just keep being kind and keep focusing.

- **Keep repeating positive affirmations** while you work and especially when things are stressful - 'I am coping… I can only do so much… I am doing wonderfully well…"

- **Start to research what jobs or careers you would love to do**. Ask yourself what do I love doing? If this can be combined with giving and helping others this will fulfil you even more.

- **By overcoming the fear you feel in your life about doing what you love you enable yourself to move forward into an amazing life**. By following the exercise Stepping Into Your Fear you will start to see that you can do anything you want in life.

Chapter Four – Questions

1. What tasks do you do on a day-to-day basis that are not adding value to you? What tasks can you delegate to others or at least share and what tasks can you drop completely?

2. Which jobs in the past have you loved doing?

3. What jobs have you always wanted to do but never got round to it? What ways can you start to research & look into these jobs – what qualifications or study do you need?

4. Write down 5 affirmations to help to inspire you at work.

5. What can you be grateful for in your current job?

CHAPTER 5
Health & Diet

Stress can have a profound effect on your health. If it is left untreated and steps are not taken to improve this, your health will be affected. Stress can cause premature ageing, headaches, muscle ache, loss of memory and many other symptoms and illnesses.

And yet we get into a routine, we get into a rhythm which as I found myself is rather hard to get out of. A senior Thai Buddhist monk once said everyone is striving for happiness. What happens, he went on, is that most people pick up the things that make themselves unhappy. Instead of picking up the things that make them happy they pick up the things that do the opposite. And the same goes for our health, we want good health but we pick up the things that make us unhealthy.

Now why is this? Why do we pick up those things that we know are bad for us? And why then afterwards do we give ourselves such a hard time? An interesting question and probably could be a book in itself.

In the West we live in a very male orientated society, a very yang, outward society. What does that mean? It means that we are more interested in striving to find the smallest atom or the furthest planet, or what everyone else is doing rather than exploring the inner world - what we feel or following what is best for us. Most women have this wonderful inner knowing, an intuition, but often times they discount this because of what everyone else is saying. Men have this quality too but it is not as pronounced and needs cultivating. How often do you think about your mother and then she calls or you get a text? Mum's do know best sometimes.

But we have slowly become detached from this intuition, this inner knowing. A mother knows when her child is sick even if the healthcare tests say otherwise. They can feel it in their gut. But as a society, this ancient form of mother-child care is dismissed as nonsense. It requires a very strong and firm woman to do what she feels is right.

So as a society we have stopped listening to our body's guidance and we now look outside of ourselves to find out whether we are healthy, what we should eat, do, be. Our bodies' know best. And when we start to listen to the inner guidance – to become aware of how it feels to eat certain things, to become aware of how it feels to exercise or to become aware of how it feels to laugh and smile, our lives radically transform.

Through the practises in this book, I hope to guide you back to knowing yourself again. Through the practises in this chapter I hope to guide you back into alignment with what you already know deep inside, what your intuition knows. But again, don't believe anything I say. This is my experience. I have found it works for me and has worked with my coaching clients, but it is your wisdom, your body knowing which will tell you whether something is right for you or not. How many diets and eating regimes are there out there? I will tell you what I have found to be helpful but you must follow what you feel suits you.

41. Exercise Is So Important For Health

Exercise is so important for your health. Humans are meant to be physical. This is how we have been for as many generations as we care to remember.

But recently there has been a shift. A shift away from the physical into the mental. The mental has its place but not at the expense of the physical. There needs to be balance.

One of the ways of getting balance in the physical is through exercise. Please study in detail the chapter on Exercise to find out what exercises are good for reducing stress. But exercise is not just great for the physical body is is also wonderful for you emotionally and mentally. Exercise really helps you ground yourself, to get out of the head and whatever stressful pattern you have locked yourself into.

Exercise allows energy to flow around the body again, and it allows any excess to be released. If you are feeling stressed or angry, going out for a walk or exercising will help to channel this energy positively.

42. Water

When we get stressed, a lot of the simple yet essential parts of our daily routine become neglected. And drinking enough water every day is one of those things.

When looking under a microscope a dehydrated cell looks like a shrivelled raisin. By contrast, a hydrated cell from a body which has drunk enough water looks like a grape. Which would you prefer to have in your body?

The average human requires 1.5 to 2 litres of water per day which is about 6-7 glasses of water. Please remember that caffeine or fizzy drinks are not counted as these drinks dehydrate rather than hydrate the body.

When working in offices I found that most people would drink 1 to 2 small cups of water a day while in the office, which was about 300ml. I found also that most people would only get water when someone else was going to the drinks machine. Few of the people I worked with seemed to have a bottle of water on their desks. If you don't drink water just be aware of what your cells are looking like and make the change. No judgement.

One of the secrets to drinking enough water is having a large enough supply of water at your desk or where you are working. Take a 1.5 to 2 litre bottle and place it next to your desk. Have a cup to drink from or drink directly from the bottle. By having a large bottle means that if you get distracted or work drags on you still have water to drink from.

What I found personally from experience is that if I don't have water at my desk or if it runs out I can go an hour or so without a drink, whereas if it is there at my desk I am constantly sipping from it.

By having a full 1.5 to 2 litre bottle at your desk at the beginning of the day means that you can then see exactly if you are drinking enough every day. I have found that drinking water is like a habit one gets into – get into the habit to sip at your bottle every ten minutes or so. Gradually you will get used to drinking more water and it will become second nature to you.

The benefits of drinking enough water are:

- Helps your kidneys to work efficiently removing toxins
- Helps to energize your muscles
- Helps to keep your skin looking good
- Helps maintain normal bowel functioning
- Can help to control calories

So by drinking enough water you help to keep the body healthy and therefore the body is more able to deal with stress as it arises.

43. Diet

Diet is a key part in maintaining health and well-being. There is a saying in the UK which was also made into a TV series which states, "You are what you eat." In other words if you eat healthily then you become healthy, if you eat poorly then you have poor health.

Most of us in the West eat a diet low on nutritional value. Due to having lifestyles which are really busy, it has created a necessity that we buy packaged and processed food. We are sold the fact that something is good for us but don't really question whether it is true or not. Everyone else is doing it so we go along with the crowd. But most of the food we eat is not really feeding us and giving us the energy and vitality that is our birthright.

To make changes in your diet will have a huge effect on your well-being. Changing your diet can have far reaching effects: clearer skin, you become fitter, weight loss, clearer thinking, improved moods, improved sleep, less prone to sickness. Diet is very powerful.

And is it true that you are what you eat? In my personal experience it is just one part of the bigger picture. What you eat is important but equally important is your relationship to it. I have known people who only ate a raw diet (only uncooked food) who were very angry and critical around food and very controlling of what they ate. All others diets were wrong. What this creates is stress. Internally you are giving yourself a hard time rather than being relaxed. This is filtered into the food. Have your known people who smoked and drank all their life only to live to their 90s. And have your heard of the fittest and healthiest people dying in their 50s.

Diet is important but as important is your relationship to it. Be relaxed around food; experiment and have fun trying different things out.

Another important thing to remember is that we are all different when it comes to food. In the Indian Ayurvedic medical system popularized by the author Deepak Chopra, they say there are 3 different categories that people fall into: light/medium/heavy – vata/pitta/kapha or a mixture of the 3 (pitta/kapha, vata/pitta for example). According to Ayurveda someone whose body make up was vata should eat a very different diet than someone whose body make up was kapha. Remember your body has great wisdom and as you eat things mindfully you will become aware of how you feel eating them: mentally, physically, and emotionally. Take note of this and with time you will find the diet for you. Experiment, try things out. Below are some pointers:

- **Avocado:** An avocado is nearly a complete food in itself. This means that it contains nearly all the food groups the body needs in order to be healthy. In certain countries avocados are mashed and fed to babies as baby food due to their high nutritional value.
- **Apricots:** Apricots are high in vitamin A.
- **Beetroot:** Beetroot is excellent for the digestive system. One way of getting the most nutrition out of a beetroot is to grate raw beetroot and carrot and mix it together as a salad or juice raw beetroot with carrots.
- **Broccoli/ Cabbage/ Cauliflower/ Brussels Sprouts:** All these vegetables are high in vitamins and minerals. The best way to cook vegetables is to steam them as this helps to keep as much of the nutrition as possible. You can also buy a juicer and juice raw vegetables and fruit together to get a high energy and vitamin drink.
  The broccoli family is known in raw food circles to be one of the healthiest foods. Adding kale, or purple sprouting broccoli to a raw juice or smoothie can be an amazing way to get all the vitamins and minerals you need in a day.
- **Brown rice:** Brown rice has more vitamins and minerals than its white counterparts. White rice is polished in order to get its whiteness which means that a lot of the vitamins and nourishment from the outside part is lost.
- **Carrots:** One carrot a day is said to contain all the vitamin A needs you would require. It is also said to have a protective effect against ultra violet rays

so this means this it helps you to look younger for longer. Adding raw grated carrots to a cooked dish before serving is a way of combing salad in your diet.

- **Chia Seeds:** These are seeds grown in South America which have high levels of vitamins and minerals. They contain Omega 3 and Omega 6 which is usually found in fish. They also contact phosphorus, calcium and magnese. Essentially they are a healthy addition to a balanced diet.

- **Cider Vinegar:** Cider vinegar helps to increase blood oxygenation, helps to strengthen your digestion and helps to increase blood clotting ability. Two teaspoons of cider vinegar in a glass of water on an empty stomach is said to be helpful in losing weight. Add cider vinegar to a grated beetroot and carrot salad for extra flavour.

- **Fruit:** Fruit is essential for a balanced and healthy diet. From bananas to strawberries, apples to pears, this food type is high in vitamins and fibre. Fruit generally digests quicker than other food types so it is best to eat fruit before a meal rather than afterwards.

- **Garlic:** Garlic has been popularized for centuries as keeping away evil spirits especially vampires. One of it's properties is helping to clean and anaesthetize wounds. In the Second World War garlic was used for exactly this purpose as an antiseptic on wounds.
  Garlic also helps to clear fat accumulations from blood vessels, lower cholesterol and protect against bacteria and viral infections.

- **Molasses:** A surprise to people but a tablespoon of black strap molasses contains as much calcium as a glass of milk. It is an alkali forming food which means that it helps to balance out foods which cause acid in the body.

- **Oats:** Oats are high in calcium, potassium and magnesium. They are also a good source of protein which helps to lower cholesterol. Having a healthy breakfast of porridge oats with fruit, nuts, seeds and dried fruit is a great way to start your day.

- **Potatoes:** Potatoes actually make the body sleepy as they contain a chemical similar to chloroform – think how you feel about a good plate of home-made mashed potatoes? They are also full of vitamins and help you to lift your mood.

- **Quinoa:** Quinoa can be used as a staple and replace rice or pasta. It is actually a seed and is very high in protein. It was considered by certain indigenous tribes in South America as valuable and was used as a currency.

- **Seeds and nuts:** Sunflower seeds, pumpkin seeds and sesame seeds are all high in vitamins and minerals. They are also excellent for hair and skin. Sesame seeds have been used for generations to treat fatigue and insomnia and they have more calcium in them than milk or cheese. Hemp seeds and linseeds (flaxseeds) are other wonderful seeds to add to your a diet. Like chia seeds they contain omega 3 and 6 and contain essential amino acids (amino acids help to break down the protein that you eat). It is best to grind seeds either in a coffee grinder or a high speed blender. Certain seeds like linseeds pass directly through the gut when in their natural state.

  Nuts like Brazil nuts, cashews, almonds, hazelnuts are a high source of protein and a good way of getting a quick energy boost – choose nuts over a bar of chocolate and you will get a sustained energy release rather than a quick high and a long low.

  I like to soak nuts and seeds in a glass jar for at least 24 hours before eating. This helps them to become more digestible. I change the water twice a day.

- **Spirulina:** Spirulina is a form of microscopic algae which under the microscope is spiral shaped hence the name. It thrives in warm alkali lakes like in Mexico and was so highly sought after by the Aztecs that they used it as currency.

  It is helpful with liver disorders and has many healing properties.

- **Sprouted Grains & Seeds:** These are a form of super food. They have been used for thousands of year, especially by the Chinese (think of bean sprouts), due to their high levels of nutrients, vitamins and minerals.

  They are high in vitamins A, C, D, E, K and B complex, in calcium, phosphorus, potassium, magnesium, iron, high quality protein and enzymes. Enzymes are especially important for your digestion and as you get older the body finds it harder to produce these. Eating sprouts therefore helps to improve your digestion and improve your metabolism for turning food into energy.

EXERCISE 27

Growing a Superfood For Health: How to grow sprouts:

You will need:

- A largish glass jar, a jar which contained 1kg of food – olives, gherkins etc.
- A piece of cheese cloth or muslin – this is very thin cotton which allows water and air to pass through it.
- Seeds and grains you can sprout: alfalfa, mung beans, lentils, chickpeas, buckwheat, sesame seeds and broccoli.

1. Place two tablespoons of grains or sprouts in the bottom of your jar. Fill it with water, cover with a piece of muslin cloth or cheese cloth (thin cotton material which lets air and water in and out) holding it on with an elastic band. Leave for at least 8 hours to soak or overnight.

2. Then drain the water off and leave in a warm, slightly lit place (certain people recommend leaving them on the windowsill but I find that they spoil more easily that way – try both ways and see which works for you).

3. Twice a day in the morning and then in the evening rinse the sprouts in cold water. Pour the water in through the cloth leaving it on, rinse it and then pour the water out through the cloth (the cloth acts as a sieve and means that you don't have to take the cloth off). Leave it to drain for 5 minutes and then shake the excess water out.

4. Leave for between 3-5 days and the sprouts should be about half a centimetre long for lentils and mung beans and about an inch long for alfafa and broccoli.

   I generally have 3 pots of sprouts on the go so that when one is finished the next lot is ready to be harvested.

You will find that certain grains and seeds take longer than others. I have personally found that the mung bean or green lentils grow the quickest and you can eat them after the sprout is about half a centimetre long.

Eat on salads, in sandwiches, in stir fries (added at the last minute to keep the nutritional value), on their own or as a snack. Enjoy!

Wheatgrass/ Barleygrass: Popularized by the author Ann Wigmore, wheatgrass has been used to heal all types of ailments. Having a similar cellular structure to blood – having 10 ml of freshly juiced wheat or barleygrass is considered similar to having a daily blood transfusion. It is high in enzymes, all vitamins and minerals, and you can either grow it yourself or buy the powdered form.

EXERCISE 28

A Power Smoothie

A smoothie is a great way of combining some of the above healthy foods into a quick and easy to make drink. This drink can then be drunk while on the go or for breakfast.

The idea for the smoothie has been on the health food circuit for a long time but I first came across it while doing physical work a few years ago. I found a heavy breakfast would give me indigestion if I cycled so I researched different sources to find a solution. I came across an athlete called Brendan Brazier who ate a raw food diet and yet still competed in Iron Man triathlons (you run a marathon, cycle 112 miles and swim 2.4 miles!) This guy was expending huge amounts of energy yet eating mainly vegetables and fruits...

I wanted to learn more and tried out his smoothie. I found drinking half a litre of smoothie before my cycle ride would give me energy but no indigestion. I was impressed. And now my breakfast consists of a fresh vegetable juice and a smoothie. Below is one of my favourite recipes:

You will need a high speed blender and the following:

- 2 Bananas
- 1 Pear
- A handful of Almonds (¼ cup of soaked almond (soak for 24 hours and then

leave in the fridge)
- ¼ cup of ground Linseeds (Flaxseeds)
- ¼ cup of ground Hemp seeds (Hemp protein)
- 8 dates
- 2 cups of salad leaves or other greens
- ½ an Avocado
- ½ a cup of sprouted pulses
- Water to taste (generally fill blender till 2-3 inches from top)

1. Place all ingredients in a nigh speed blender. Fill water to 2-3 inches from top and blend. Easy, easy, easy. Some blenders are smaller so decrease quantities as needed or blend 2 separate batches and then mix.

2. And then enjoy – you can keep topping it up with water as you drink it so the smoothie lasts longer.

44. Relaxation Time

A really important part of managing your stress levels and therefore helping your health is to have relaxation time or down time. It is really important to have a holiday from time to time, but it is also really important to schedule in relaxation time every week and where possible every day. This might seem an impossible task for some of you – I can hear you saying, "but do you know how busy I am?" Well, yes I do know how busy you are but I also know that without having relaxation time you are not really running to the maximum of your ability.

Those of you who work from home will notice that it is very easy for your work to spill over into other areas of your life. And this is especially the case if you and your partner are in the same business. One of my best friends runs his business from home and he has often told me that his home space doesn't feel like home but like work.

So whether you work from home or you work in an office it is so important to have down time – time where you switch off from work and relax.

I personally feel that most people need at least a day's break from work a week. This means that you don't think about business, you don't talk about it, you don't switch on your computer and you don't answer business calls.

The reason I recommend that people take a day off at the weekend is for the reason that most other people are off work and therefore less likely to call you. By taking relaxation time for yourself once a week you allow the mind to do an amazing thing. Because we have many levels to our consciousness – subconscious, unconscious, supra consciousness when we rest and stop thinking about things on a conscious level our thoughts are still being ordered on an unconscious and subconscious level.

What this means is that by giving yourself time for your consciousness to order your thoughts you gain clarity and get your best inspiration after this down time. Ideas pop into your mind and you get inspiration for new ideas.

The trick is just not think about it, this only really works when you are not focusing on work and are resting, relaxing and having fun.

So this is why it is important to rest – to not only relax the body and mind but also to help you gain clarity in your thoughts. For example, think of days at work where you hadn't slept much the night before – how much clarity did you have?

And when you have rested well, feel relaxed and calm how do you feel then? And how much better are you able to focus on the job in hand?

So having a day's relaxation time once a week is imperative not only for your health and in order to reduce your stress levels but also to help you to achieve all that you want in life – for when you have clarity you know the path to walk and the doors to open…

45. The Power of Visualisation

A key to obtaining better health is the clarity of your vision. We have spoken before when talking of the Vision Movie of the importance of working out what you do want. Well, this also applies in relation to your health. What do you want in terms of your health? How do you want to feel physically? What is your vision for your health?

The key in visualisation is seeing what you want e.g. being very fit and doing physical sports and feeling great while doing it. It is essential to have these 2 aspects – the vision and the feeling. If you are visualising something, like great health, but, for example, the idea of running 10 miles fills you with dread then it is unlikely to come to pass. You must visualise what you want and then feel great about your vision.

The third aspect of visualisation when it comes to health is to do with belief, faith, or certainty. Your job is to truly believe that what you are envisioning in the mind has already come to pass, that it is a reality on one level. You have so much certainty that e.g. your health is amazing, that you feel great now.

And if you get lost looking at the present reality, saying but I am not healthy, I am overweight, remember to keep coming back to the vision and the feeling. The power of the mind is amazing; anything created in this world was firstly envisioned in the mind first. All the amazing inventions which no one thought possible, like the light bulb, or the airplane started this way. The Wright brothers used to say to each other when another of their inventions failed - "It's all right brother, I can see myself riding in that machine, and it travels easily and steadily." And indeed it was.

So your job with your health is not to get swayed from your vision. When it would seem that your health is not so good, keep going back to your vision, see yourself as well, know yourself as well. Keep remembering that your health is the way it is in the present due to all the thoughts you have thought until now – your past thoughts. The thoughts you think now will create a new reality, a new picture of health and well-being.

And this leads to the 4th step – the actions. When you have your vision of your health, you feel the feelings of this great health and you feel the certainty that it is on it's way, or that it is already here you will be inspired to do things – like go to the local gym, join the local dance class, go to the mediation class, or start buying raw foods.

And when you get that inspiration – act on it. Yes, follow it through. You have created the ideal picture in your mind and now the possibilities are unfolding before your eyes. In fact, you might not need to do much, the way will be shown to you.

Add pictures to your Vision Movie of what you look like in your ideal scenario, what you are eating in your ideal life and watch this once a day. In any spare moments keep visualising what you do want and the good feelings that flow from this. And it will amaze you how quickly your health will become amazing.

46. The Gift of Laughter

Laughter is amazing. It is one of the greatest gifts we can offer ourselves in terms of healing the body, mind and spirit. There have been many stories over the years of some high profile people healing themselves of illness through the use of laughter. One such case is Norman Cousins who was a political journalist, and author. He was diagnosed with several illnesses but managed to live much longer than the doctors predicted by watching Marx Brother's film. He said:

"I made the joyous discovery that ten minutes of genuine belly laughter had an anesthetic effect and would give me at least two hours of pain-free sleep. When the pain-killing effect of the laughter wore off, we would switch on the motion picture projector again and not infrequently, it would lead to another pain-free interval."

I have used the power of laughter in my own life and when working with clients. I first started to practise laughter yoga, which is a set of exercises to induce laugher, when I had been going through a stressful time. I realised that I was being too serious so looked online at different ways of dealing with this. I came across laughter yoga and have been practising it ever since.

The idea behind laughter yoga is to force laughter for a period of time through doing exercises. What the founder of Laughter Yoga, Dr Madan Kataria, found is that you still got all the health benefits of laughter even if it was forced. These include:

- Boosting the immune system
- Laughter release endorphins, the body's natural feel good chemicals which make you feel great and also relieve pain.

- Laughter protects the heart through improving the function of blood vessels and increasing blood flow
- Laughter relaxes the whole body
- Lower stress levels.

I love laughter and practise laughter yoga 4 or 5 times a week even if it is just for 10 minutes. I feel very alive, very happy and energized after doing my laughter sessions. I also feel more clarity and am able to let go of any worries or complaints I might have – I realise that they are just not important.

EXERCISE 29

Laughter Shaking

The following exercise can be done with other people or on your own.

1. Stand or sit with your back straight and your feet shoulder width apart.

2. Raise your right hand to head height. Start to shake your arm and hand, and start laughing. Feel the laughter filling your body from the feet to the crown of the head. Laugh for about 30 seconds. It is okay to force it – you will still gain the above benefits and eventually the laughter will become natural and you won't be able to stop...

3. Repeat with your left hand while feeling the laughter filling the body.

4. Then lastly repeat with both hands and arms raised. Shake the whole body.

5. Then rest. Press the thumb and 2nd fingertips together for 10 seconds. Feel the endorphins running round your system healing your heart, organs and improving blood flow. Feel how good it feels to be alive and well – it really is a rush!

I really love this exercise and had great fun doing it just know. Try it and see how it feels to have endorphins running round your whole body! If you have concerns about what you will look like to others do it on your own.

47. Use Smiling To Improve Your Health

Smiling is another of those "things" that we often forget as we get into the busyness and stress of our everyday lives. We retreat to our minds and for some reason we forget to see that there are others around us. We notice how much we've got to do, and how busy we are and can rush around barking orders at people. In return, those people can be quite blunt with us.

What smiling does is it reconnects us to other people. A simple smile can melt the barriers that we have with other people. When I worked corporately after the monastery I smiled at everyone in the office. And it felt lovely. People really appreciate being smiled at – well, it gives them a chance to smile back. For some people it is a shock at first so they don't smile back – they're not used to it, but persevere and they will smile at you. Smile from your heart – feel your heart overflowing as you smile – a real heartfelt smile. And what this does is it really improves the vibe in the office or where you live or with your family or in your town. There is one man in my own town who bounces around and smiles at everyone – it is lovely.

The other thing about smiling is that it is really good for your health. Just as laughter is great medicine, so likewise is smiling. The health benefits of smiling are:

- Opens the sinus passageways through the contraction of the cheek muscles. This is turn allows more blood flow into the brain which helps to reduce stress through cooling the blood in the brain. When the blood in the brain gets too hot we can become angry and snappy.
- When the sinus passageways open through smiling it also makes it easier to breathe.
- Releases endorphins, feel good hormones into the bloodstream.
- Improves sleeping, especially when smiling is practised at night-time.
- It is a very easy and inexpensive way to feel good.

According to Mantak Chia, the Taoist teacher, in his book Transform Stress into Vitality, he suggests that smiling is directly related to the thymus gland. The thymus gland lives in the centre of your chest the second rib down below the throat. In the Taoist system the thymus gland is the seat of greater enlightenment, the seat of love and the seat of life force chi energy. What this essentially means is the thymus gland is an extremely important part of your body for emotional, physical and spiritual health. When we are under stress the thymus gland is the first to be affected. Think about it – how do you feel when you are stressed? Do you feel loving, energized and spiritually awake?

John Diamond, M.D., in his book Your Body Doesn't Lie, writes about a study showing that the thymus gland has a role as the master controller that directs life-giving and healing energies of the body. The Nobel Prize Winner, Sir MacFarlane Burnet, suggests that increasing the activity of the thymus gland will result in a greater ability to ward off cancer.

It is suggested in Taoism that when you smile your internal organs release a honey like secretion (Mantak Chia) which nourishes the whole body. Smiling into your organs also helps your organs to expand so that they become soft and moist improving efficiency and a deeper sense of relaxation in your body.

On the other hand, in Taoism it is also suggested that when you are feeling negative emotions like fear or anger the organs release a poisonous secretion which can cause insomnia, increased blood pressure and loss of appetite.

Essentially, it is important to smile. The following exercise which is based on Mantak Chia's inner smile exercise will help you to increase the activity of the thymus, expand your organs and improve your overall health. As with all the exercises in this book, try it out for a period of time and see how it affects you. Let your body be the judge of how well a practise is for you. Your job is just to turn up and do the exercise on a daily basis. The body's job is to tell you how an exercise feels after doing it.

EXERCISE 30

Inner Smile

PLEASE READ THROUGH THE WHOLE EXERCISE BEFORE YOU START.

1. Find a quiet spot at least an hour after eating food. It is best to be wearing warm, comfortable clothing. Sit on the edge of a chair with your back straight and your hands on your lap clasped together one on top of the other, legs shoulder width apart.

2. Breathe naturally. Relax your forehead. Start to imagine meeting someone you deeply love or seeing a beautiful sight (maybe a memory from one of the other exercises in this book).

3. **Front Line:** We will first of all smile down the front line of organs. Allow the energy of love to start to flow into the midpoint between the eyes and then down imagine it flowing down into the face, relaxing the face muscles, the jaw, the facial skin, the nose, the cheeks. Allow the energy to flow inside your face relaxing the muscles so that your jaw drops and all tension drops away. Bring your tongue to the roof of your mouth so that it is touching the palate (90 degrees up) and leave it there for the duration of the exercise.

4. Allow this feeling to flow down your neck, throat and shoulders bringing warmth and relaxation there. Allow the sensation to flow down into your thymus and then to your heart – filling your heart with joy. You can remember the memory or the visual at this time to increase the feeling of joy.

5. Bring this energy into the lungs now – thanking the lungs for the amazing job that they do. Feel them filling with a warm and nurturing glow. Now allow this love, and joy to flow down into the liver bringing kindness and feeling it softening and growing moister.

6. Allow this energy to overflow now into the kidneys and the adrenal glands. Feel them filling with this smiling energy and overflowing with joy, love, courage, kindness and gentleness.

7. Now feel the energy overflowing into the pancreas, spleen and then into the genital area. Feeling love and joy permeating these important parts of the body.

8. Return to the eyes and now quickly smile down the front line of organs again releasing any remaining tension.

9. **Middle Line:** Now we will smile down the middle line. Become aware again of the smiling energy in your eyes – remember meeting a person you love or an amazing memory. Let it flow down into your mouth and your saliva. Touching the tongue to the roof of the mouth now swallow loudly following the smiling energy down your oesophagus into your stomach. Thank your stomach for the amazing work it does digesting your food.

10. Allow this wonderful smiling feeling to flow down your small intestine and then into your large intestine. Return to your eyes and then quickly smile down the middle line again releasing any tension.

11. **Back Line:** Bring your attention and the smiling energy back to your eyes. Smile inwards with both eyes allowing the energy to pool in your mid eyebrow area. Move the smiling energy into the whole left side of the brain moving the energy back and forth and then repeating this on the right side of the brain allowing both sides of the brain to become balanced and aligned.

12. Now spiral this energy from the eyes backwards until you reach the spine. Start to smile down each vertebra of the spine bringing warmth and relaxation. Feel the spine elongating and expanding so that you feel taller.

13. Now return the energy to the eyes and quickly smile down the complete back line.

14. Come back to the eyes and smile down all these lines – front, middle and back, at once. Feel the energy cascading down you like a waterfall of joy, love and appreciation. You are loved – deeply.

15. Now bring your focus to your navel – the tan tien, the one point, and focus the energy there so that it collects in your navel. You have now finished the inner smile – well done!

Be patient with this exercise. It is long but it is a very powerful healer. To start with you can do abbreviated forms of this exercise speeding it up if you feel the need. But the most benefit gained from this exercise will be when done fully. This is not the complete Taoist Inner Smile as taught by Mantak Chia – that is much longer, but for our purposes this abbreviated form will bring much relaxation, healing and joy.

It was February 2000 and things were rolling sluggishly along. I was going back to visit my father from time to time but there didn't seem much haste in seeing him as we hadn't learned of the terminal nature of his illness yet.

My new job was a bit unbelievable really. I found it terribly boring. My role was to trawl through hundreds of pages of official documentation for syndicated loans and find some interesting and important information with which to then write an article. I did it but didn't know what I was doing or about what I was writing about. I had been in the same situation 2 years before when I had first started work selling corporate leasing courses. I knew a bit about leasing from my International Business degree but very little. The saving grace with working in sales had been talking to humans on the phone. This new job had very little contact with others, apart from my colleagues.

My health was pretty poor at this time. I did very little exercise. I remember going to the swimming pool locally in Kentish Town one day and nearly drowning because I was so unfit. I walked to and from the local station in the morning and evening but that was it. I was eating and drinking poorly – lots of bacon, sausages, cheese, milk, alcohol, coffee, drugs. I felt pretty sluggish and hazy really. I wasn't taking care of myself at all – I didn't have the time or energy – or so I thought...

My relationship was ticking along. My partner was an amazing person – very kind, loving, generous, intelligent and very devoted to me. She was working in banking and was very talented at her job (contacting her recently I realise that she is now a Vice President of an international bank – makes me see what different path I could have taken). And seeing where she is now I realise that she was committed to working in London. I spoke to her at the time about moving out of London and she said that she would be happy to commute in and live on the outskirts.
One day I made an off-hand remark which upset her. I apologised and went off to Hampstead Heath with my writing book. I found a bench and started to write.

I had no idea what would come out of me but I started to write a poem about what was happening in my relationship. The result was amazing. It shocked me. It stunned me. The poem had come to the conclusion that I should leave my partner! What! I can't do that, but I went back to my flat and told my partner that I would be leaving her.

She was absolutely dumbfounded, devastated and then angry at me. Our relationship had been so smooth really – we never argued and had so much in common, but this was my guidance, I needed to leave. She was shocked but I explained that it was nothing to do with her. I was confused, I needed to find out who I was and I also was questioning my sexuality at the time – thinking that I might be gay. Yes, literally I was throwing myself off the cliff and had no idea what was about to happen...

But deep down I knew that I didn't love her, in fact, I didn't love anything or anyone – I was emotionally shut down. I had to go. So 2 weeks after telling my partner it was over, I left our apartment in Tufnell Park in North London never to return. I was devastated but I knew I had many questions I needed answering...

Recap for Health & Diet

- Remember that **unchecked stress will affect your health**, and the longer you leave it the more the affects can increase.
- **Exercise is one of the main stress relieving tools**. Exercise helps you to get into the body, balance the mind and emotions and promotes well-being.
- **You are what you eat** – eat well and you get the health benefits but eat unhealthily and you increase the levels of stress you place on your body.
- **Having time to relax and unwind helps to uncoil the stresses and strains** that have build up over the week. Have at least one day of down time a week.
- **Visualisation** is a powerful tool for regaining health. By focusing on how you do want your health to be and feeling those amazing feelings will take a great weight off your body.
- **Laughter and smiling** heal. The evidence is strong to suggest that smiling and laughing everyday will change your life. Try it and see. Smile at those around you. Laugh with your loved ones!

Chapter Five – Questions

1. Name five foods that will help you to reduce stress.

2. How often would it be good to have relaxation time in a week?

3. What exercise or exercises did you choose to engage in from chapter one? Write down 3 more steps which will help to get your goal fulfilled – visualize them and then do them.

4. What are the health benefits of laughter and smiling?

CHAPTER 6

Holiday Stress & Time Off

Holiday times should be a time of relaxation, calm and peace. Holidays should be a time where you unwind and recuperate from day to day life.

But for many of us, our holidays are just as stressful if not more stressful than day to day living. It's as if we carry our everyday stress into our holidays.

And we seem to work extra hard just before our holidays so that we can get everything done. By the time the holiday arrives we are burnt out. And because we have worked so hard for the previous year we find it really hard to let go at holiday times. In fact, sometimes we are really looking forward to getting back to work just to get away from our loved ones, or families.

So how do you turn this around so that holiday times become a time of rest and relaxation? How do your turn this around so that on holiday you are able to let go and give your body the time it needs to be at rest? What can you do to make sure your holidays are peaceful and stress-free?

46. Have Regular Time Off

A key to having holidays where you can relax and unwind is having regular time off. Rather than only having a few weeks off a year, you start to have time off regularly. This means that when you get to your holiday you are already well-versed in relaxation so that your holiday is of great benefit to you. In fact, it is just an extension of the amazing life that you are now living – relaxed, flowing, doing what you love.

The well-being way is a journey not a destination. Often times with holidays we see them as the destination. I'll just do this one more project and then I'll have a holiday. I'll do this one more thing before I have a break. The key point here is making the journey relaxing rather than expecting that the destination will be relaxing. Indeed, it has been mentioned before in this book that if the journey is stressful then it is most probable that the destination will be stressful too.

In our society there is so much pressure to go to the "right" place, to have the "right" holiday. We stress ourselves out on the journey to get the right holiday and then wonder why we don't enjoy ourselves. So what do you do?

The first thing in order to find balance in your life, and on the journey is that you start to have regular time off. This means not doing anything at least once a week: resting, sleeping, doing things you enjoy. This means not picking up work or doing chores in the house.

I personally see my weekends as a holiday. It is a time that I don't work in the office. I stop. I rest, I watch a film or go for a walk or I spend time pottering in the garden. I meet friends or I sleep till midday. I do the things that I need to do to unwind. If I am working on the weekends then I make sure I get a day off during the week where I do something different.

But how do I do that if I have a family to look after? This means flowing with your family rather than against it. Are you always doing what your children or your partner wants to do? What about your needs and wants? Are they being met?

If you love walking well, suggest it to your family. I have found in my own case that the children I have looked after are always reluctant to go into nature to start off with. They want to sit at home and watch TV. So turn the TV off and take them out to a park or a lake.
They might well dig their heels in to start off with but don't let that put you off. People dig their heels in when they have to step out of their comfort zone. And what you find will happen, as I found myself, is that the kids love it. They enjoy themselves so much and so do you.

See spending time with your family as a holiday. Enjoy their presence. Yes, enjoy every moment of play or doing magical things. I have always found when looking after children that when I tried to answer emails or do other non-children related things that I used to become irritated because they would always interrupt me during this time. What I learned was that in order not to get stressed I had to give my 100% attention to them. That meant that I could sit on the sofa while they watched a film but wouldn't watch it myself. I knew that when I got engrossed in the film they would get distracted and start making lots of noise and I would feel annoyed. I needed to be 100% present. Try this with your family. Rather than thinking about work or trying to fit things in, be totally present with them. And it will feel like a complete holiday for you.

Secondly, it is important to have a break once a day. Yes, spend 30 minutes on waking, or in the evening doing some of the practises in this book – like meditation or yoga, or tai chi. Again, by taking this time for yourself you are literally having a holiday every day. And the body loves this. The mind might struggle to start off with, but just allowing the whole body to stop for 30 minutes – just sitting, going nowhere, fills you up. You keep filling yourself up and wellness spreads throughout your body.

47. Have a Few Days After Your Holiday To Acclimatise

How often do you come back from holiday on the eve before your return to work? How often are you still tired or even jet lagged when you start back at work? Have you ever heard yourself saying after coming back from holiday, "I need another holiday now!"

Manage your holiday so that you have a few days after you return from a trip away to acclimatise. Things like washing or ironing need to be done before starting work, so give yourself a few days to settle into your home routine again. Not only will this give you some time to relax before you go back to work but it will also get you focused and ready for work again.

By not taking this time it can feel like a big shock going back to work. By the end of the first day you may well hear yourself saying, "I need another holiday!" So take a few days to reacclimatise before you start back at work. Be gentle, be kind.

48. If You Go Abroad Be Aware Of Others' Customs And Habits

Foreign countries or even unknown places can be stressful for some people. Remember this when booking a holiday. If you are prone to getting anxious when people don't speak your language or you can get frustrated with "different" customs book your destination with this in mind.

Some people love to be in new locations as this can be exciting for them but for others this can be even more stressful. If this is the case then book something in your own country, or in a place which speaks English or your mother tongue fluently.

I remember travelling in Europe in the 90s. I was travelling in the south of France and then I went into Spain. I could speak French but not Spanish. So as soon as I went over the border into Spain I found it frustrating. People couldn't understand me and it was difficult to get what I wanted.

I remember feeling frustrated with the customs and feeling out of place. But as soon as I went back into France… it was like coming home again. People could understand me and I didn't feel a stranger. I felt relaxed and at peace. I started to enjoy myself again.

Sure I had seen some wonderful things in Spain but it wasn't the same to being in a country where people could understand me.

So I would offer this advice to you when choosing a destination. If you are likely to get stressed or frustrated because people don't understand you, choose again.

Remember, a holiday is for de-stressing not for adding to your stress.

But if you are a person who loves the excitement of learning new customs and languages then do go abroad. If you love being taken out of your comfort zone then go where you will be challenged. Often times you will learn the most and have the most amazing experiences when you step out of your comfort zones, but remember that you holiday is for relaxation, being at ease and allowing the body, mind and spirit some recuperation time.

49. Have Time To Rest On Holiday

Again this might seem very obvious but I know many of my friends who will go on holiday and get very little rest. They will spend time sightseeing, or partying, or visiting family… and do very little resting.

The needs of others will be filled but not their own. And what does this lead to? More stress and more frustration which is then carried back into the scenario of, "I need another holiday!"

What is suggested to people is that if you are going on holiday for 2 weeks have at least a week where you do nothing, sit on a beach, go walking, doing things to feed yourself, doing things to replenish your batteries – eating, resting and playing well.

When I go on holiday I generally will spend the first week unwinding, usually sat on a beach resting and sunbathing and then swimming and surfing. What this does for me is to replenish my batteries. I can then go sightseeing if I want to but only once I have replenished myself.

By resting you allow your body and mind to stop. You might feel fine but once you allow yourself to stop you can then gauge - "Wow, actually I am so tired – I just need to sleep and snooze by a pool for a few days." Settle in gently to your holiday – you have worked hard, so take it easy, be gentle with your self.

50. Have Time On Your Own

Many of you might find that being with your partner or spouse constantly while on holiday can be a struggle. Why is this?

When we are at home we get into routines. We work, rest, have our activities with the family and the activities when we are away from the family. But if truth be told we don't actually spend that much time with our partners, children or spouses.

What this creates is that when you go on holiday suddenly you are spending time with people who you haven't really spent much quality time with over the past year. And although this is much needed it can sometimes be too much and become stressful.

So what would I suggest?

Firstly, I would say that it is important that you and your partner agree to have days where you do things separately – maybe one of you takes the kids while the other rests. Or visit places which really appeal to one and not the other separately.

By doing this you create space to truly appreciate and see the beauty in the other partner. This is why I say that meditation is so important. Meditation helps to settle and clear the mind. It allows the mind clarity so that it can see the woods from the trees, it can see the truth in a situation rather getting lost in the drama.

This is what you do when you take time apart to nourish yourself – you start to see clearly.

"Nourish yourself fully so that you can then feed others."

51. Nourish Yourself On Holiday

Nourishing your on holiday means giving to you. It means sleeping in, resting or doing what you love. It means taking time to be still or to exercise – it means listening to what you need on all levels and then giving yourself those things. Turn your mobile or laptop off (or don't take it at all) and leave them off. See that and know that everything will be well while you are on holiday. Everything externally will be taken care of so your task on holiday is taking care of you.

When you nourish yourself like this and when you relax deeply like this you are replenishing the batteries so that you will have so much to give when you return to everyday life. You will be filled to overflowing. The following exercise will help to nourish you on a deep level:

EXERCISE 31

Stopping

You have arrived on holiday. You have got to your destination. Or it is your first day of holiday at home. You are tired but you want to explore, do things and your family feel the same.

But wait…

Stop…

Spend several days at your location doing… yes you got it… nothing!

If there is a pool or a beach, set an intent that…

"I give myself permission to unwind…."
"I give myself permission to let go of any worries or fears and relax!
"I breathe in and I enjoy myself today because I am allowing myself to stop…"

And feel the tension of the year or since you last had a holiday slip away from you.

And let your children and family do the same thing. Stay at the hotel for a few days – the kids can run around the pool and make friends while you and your beloved can stop. Yes, stop.

What you will find is that your holiday is the best you have ever had by doing this exercise. Why? What is so great about this method?

Well, what happens is that you approach the holiday and what you do within it from a balanced and rested perspective. You take a few days break and then you acknowledge how you are feeling and from there you and your family organise what you want to do from this perspective. If you rest for a few days and then you all realise that you feel tired and burnt out then you say "we will do very little this holiday". If after a few days rest you feel energized and ready to go make choices of what you want to do from there. Organise things to do around that.

What a lot of people do is that they arrive on holiday really tired but because they are in an amazing place want to do lots of things. Rather than rest they tire themselves out even further. By doing the above technique you work out how you are feeling – am I really tired and need to rest? By *stopping* first you then do things from a balanced perspective rather than from a stressed out and hectic place.

So next time you are on holiday or even at the weekend try this *stopping* exercise.

52. How To Deal With Xmas and Family Gatherings

I once met a very wise man who told me something which helped me tremendously at the time and has helped me ever since.

He said that our families are our ultimate teachers. For no matter how "enlightened" or magical you feel, your family has the ability to trigger your "stuff", your "baggage". They challenge you, say things which no one else would dare to say or make you feel like a small child again.

So this means that family gatherings and Xmases can be really challenging. I have certainly had challenging Xmases and many things have been brought up for me. One year I couldn't stop crying for 3 days after having a huge argument with my mother. But through these experiences I have learned many things.

So what is the solution to this?

53. Keep Your Stress Management Practise Going

Use the well-being tools throughout this book like meditation and compassion to keep yourself balanced. The truth is that sometimes we can't be bothered to do things that we know will help us. We are stubborn, we won't accept the help of others or our own help.

But this has consequences and the more we awaken to ourselves and our patterns we start to see that there is a cause and an effect.

What does this mean?

Let's take an example. You are at home at Xmas. You know that if you meditate, do some exercise, spend some time on your own then Xmas will go well.

But you forget to do this or you can't be bothered.

So your Xmas turns out really tough – your family are having a go at you, you end up shouting at them and walking out on them.

The **cause** is doing the stress relief tools or not.

The **effect** is the result of what you put in.

At a training course I was running with my wife one of the participants asked how long it took to be good at meditation. And the answer?

How much time do you want to devote to it? How much time do you want to spend doing these stress relief techniques? Make time for them and they will make time for you. If you want to be fit – does running for 5 miles once a month get your fit? Put the practise in and you will get the rewards.

EXERCISE 32

Whole Body Relaxation Technique

1. Find yourself a nice, peaceful spot where you will not be disturbed. Sit comfortably or lie down. It is worth setting your alarm for 30 minutes if you have something to do afterwards (you might fall asleep).

2. Take a few deep breaths. Breathe in and breathe out. Relax your body. Breathe in and breathe out.

3. Start to focus on your head. Allow it to soften and for any tension in your muscles to be released. Feel all thoughts being let go of. Keep breathing deeply at all times.

4. Imagine that as you breathe out that you breathe your thoughts into the earth.

5. Move down to your shoulders – soften, relax and feel peace in your shoulders. Breathe in and out with your attention focused on your shoulders. Stay there breathing for a few minutes.

6. Then move down to the arms and hands and do the same. Now repeat the process throughout your whole body spending a few minutes on each area: upper chest, internal organs, lower stomach, upper and lower back, buttocks, upper legs - thighs, calves, ankles and feet.

7. Then breathe into the whole body. Relaxing the whole body. Feel yourself breathing into your body as a whole – all the parts you have relaxed all together.

8. This should last about 20 minutes. After doing this exercise gradually open your eyes and move your body.

This exercise is deeply relaxing and you could use this exercise as part of your daily holiday routine we spoke about before. This exercise helps to relax and rejuvenate the body, mind and emotions. A great exercise for a challenging time. You will have more perspective and clarity after this exercise.

54. Have Compassion For Your Family And Don't Get Drawn In

Compassion is a really powerful way of allowing your heart to open towards your family and possibly heal that which needs to be healed. By having compassion with your family, relatives and loved one means that you don't get drawn in. It is almost like you have this space inside which means that you don't react, you see and hear what they are saying or doing but don't pulled in. So how do you cultivate this compassion?

The first thing to do is to acknowledge that you are doing fine. Although you might feel tense and nervous or upset, you are doing just fine. Remember, be gentle with yourself. It is time to stop giving yourself a hard time about your family – giving yourself a hard time over what you "should" say or do or how you should be. First thing, be gentle with yourself. For if you are calm and peaceful and not bothered by anything then this rubs off on others. If you are angry and stressed, again, this too rubs off on others.

Secondly, start to cultivate compassion within you. The below exercise will help you on your way to cultivating this important jewel within. The jewel is there already – what this exercise does is start to recognise and take care of it.

EXERCISE 33

Having Compassion For Others

To be done on your own as a practise (to be done only when you are in a good space):

1. Close your eyes. Go back to a situation in your life that was a little challenging or painful – a memory that was slightly unsettling (nothing too intense). Briefly go back to this time.

2. Feel how you feel. Feel the suffering you felt. Feel your heart opening. Feel the feeling that you would not want anyone else to go through this same pain.

3. And draw a picture in your mind's eye of those closest to you. See them and truly feel that you would not want them to suffer as you have suffered. May they be free of all suffering.

4. And then draw a picture in your mind's eye of those who are annoying you and you don't like. Feel how they feel to act and do the things to annoy you. They are probably suffering when they hurt you. And make the wish that they be well too. You know what it feels like to suffer in your heart and make the wish that they be free from suffering as well.

To be done in a challenging situation (as it arises):

1. You are confronted with someone and you are starting to feel challenged – maybe this person is angry, upset or annoyed). Take a deep breath.

2. Become aware that they are suffering to be saying, doing or acting in this way. They are hurting just like you have really hurt in the past. Remember your practise above about cultivating compassion and make the wish that they not suffer as you have suffered in the past. Repeat, "May you be well, may you be well, may you be well" under your breath.

3. Where possible say nothing or if your feel totally centred in your love and compassion for the other person say something appropriate.

4. See a bubble of electric blue light around yourself at arms length and around the other person. See their discomfort healing while you keep your heart open and inside your bubble.

5. You will find the situation will resolve itself gently and peacefully.

55. Do Breathing Techniques When Things Get Challenging

When all else fails count to 10. How many times have you heard this? Have you ever done this yourself or know someone who has actually done this? Well, very few of us do this. Very few of us breathe. Take a deep breath in now and relax, relax now while you are reading this. Breathe deeply and relax. Let go. Allow your shoulders to drop and to relax. Breathe in deeply.... and then breathe out deeply... Feels good doesn't it?

Well, breathing deeply helps us to get perspective. If you imagine your stress relief practise being like a house, then your meditation practise is like the bricks, and your breathing techniques and the other tools in this book are like the cement. Your breathing and the various tools keep the house standing.

This analogy of the house is useful in that each part is important. Sitting and meditating twice a day is extremely important, but this formal part of the practise is not practised all day unless you are on meditation retreat. Therefore something needs to fill in the gaps. This is your breathing practise, your tools. As you develop your practise you will find that life can become like a meditation in that every action is peaceful and mindful.

Breathing techniques help you to centre you in this moment. To get clarity in this moment. Now. Here. Right here, right now.

Feel how you feel now if you breathe deeply while reading this? The following exercise is very quick and can be used with visiting family members or with colleagues.

EXERCISE 34

Counting to 10

So you are at home at Xmas. Your mother-in-law is visiting or some other relation that challenges you.

She or they keep saying things that you feel are undermining you or putting you down. You are starting to seethe, to get angry and are just waiting for the moment to pounce with some really nasty comment.

Catch yourself at this moment.

1. Breathe in … Breathe out… one
2. Breathe in … Breathe out… two.. I am a good person
3. Breathe in … Breathe out… three…I feel what I am feeling
4. Breathe in … Breathe out… four… this feeling is mine
5. Breathe in … Breathe out… five… I take responsibility for how I feel.
6. Breathe in … Breathe out… six… I am powerful and strong
7. Breathe in … Breathe out… seven… I am a good person whatever I feel others are saying.
8. Breathe in … Breathe out… eight… I am relaxed because I am in control of my emotions
9. Breathe in … Breathe out… nine… I am in control
10. Breathe in … Breathe out… ten… I am balanced and calm

Try this exercise now…

Try it because through practice when you need it most it will be there for you…

Remember what you put in you get out as effects…

How did you find the exercise? The amazing thing with this exercise is that not only will you say nothing to your mother-in-law or your relation but they will sense a change in you. For some reason they will stop putting you down. And if they don't, well, you will just have this huge space of joy in your heart and feel compassion that they feel so unhappy to criticise and put you down.

56. Some Stress Is Okay

What do I mean by that? Well, sometimes the most enjoyable things require a little stress to start off with.

Have you ever been skydiving? Well, if you haven't can you imagine how that feels to be in the plane before hand? Stressful and probably very unpleasant – your stomach is in knots and heart is racing so fast that you think that it will jump right out of your chest.

This is good stress. This tells us there is a dangerous situation around the corner which requires us to be on alert.

But then we jump and get the buzz of the skydive. And afterwards we feel elated and so glad that we pushed through the short term stress that we were feeling.

Some stress is required in order for us to be functioning as human beings, to get us out of bed in the morning.

But the main point of a holiday is to reduce these levels of stress so you can recuperate physically, mentally and emotionally. But a little stress is okay. So don't give yourself a hard time if you don't manage to eliminate all stress while you are on holiday do what you can...

So here I was, in the early part of the year 2000, in London having just started a new job but now I had no where to live. I hadn't thought this through, of course, any reasonable person would have thought about the consequences before making the jump. Some people would have thought it through a little more before quitting their home and partner of 4 years. But sometimes it is just not like that. Sometimes it is time to jump off the cliff and see what happens.

I am sure I could have chosen an easier way. I am sure I could have thought this through. Indeed 13 years on with a lot, and I mean a lot of water having passed under the bridge, I would have acted differently. I see now in my present relationship that it is so much better to work things through. But I didn't have this hindsight 13 years ago. Indeed, I was an emotional wreck at that time but was in complete denial of it. The events of the following few years would help to shake the foundations and clear this inner household of what I was carrying.

And what was I carrying? At the time I didn't know, all that I knew was that I was starting to struggle. Pretty much from the time I left my partner I started to have a breakdown. Feelings that I had previously suppressed started to bubble up to the surface. There were times when I thought that I was going crazy. And on one level I was – by rational means, by the norm, I was doing some crazy things – quitting my partner when there was nothing wrong, having no idea what I was going to do.

A friend from school, the only friend from school, offered me a couch to sleep on, and potentially a bed if one of his flatmates didn't come home at night... I took him up on the offer – there was nowhere else to go and still keep my job. I have to admit that the situation was not ideal. My friend was still at medical school and lived with 3 other medical students. Students have a habit of being pretty messy. Some in the house did clean up but seemed to have given up cleaning up after others so the kitchen sink was usually full of dishes.

I was grateful for the roof over my head and sometimes the bed, but the sheets hadn't been washed for months so it didn't improve how I was feeling. In the evenings I ate in fast food restaurants on my own. I felt terribly lonely. I really didn't know what I had done or why the hell I had done it. My family over the next year or so pointed out that I would be better getting back together with my ex. But that wasn't the point. I had to find out about me.

I slept on the couch for a few weeks, and then I house sat for a friend while they were on holiday. After about a month of doing this I was feeling pretty depressed. The job was not lifting my spirits and to be honest there wasn't anything else. I felt suicidal. My sister then suggested that I move in with her. It was like a breath of fresh air. I couldn't have survived much longer couch surfing in the emotional state I was in. My sister lived near to Guildford, south of London and the idea of my own bed and a place of my own seemed like heaven. Whether I worked this out at the time, or later on but the commuting journey was 4 hours both ways! I tried to meditate on the journey but didn't really succeed.

One day in the office, a friend called to ask if he could see my ex. My partner and I had had no contact since splitting up and both of us wanted to keep it that way until we had both done some healing. Hearing this from my friend devastated me. I felt betrayed – did he want to date her, what was his game? I felt really angry and upset.

On the journey back to my sister's that night I cried continually staring out of the window. I felt so devastated that I didn't care that this was a rush-hour train and I had 4 to 6 people sat opposite me trying not to watch me. I couldn't go on. I'd had enough. I decided then and there to end it. I had nothing. I had left everything that was important to me and the job, well, that just added to the hopelessness of the situation.

I managed to get back to my sister's town and sat in the park willing myself to go through with the suicide. But I just couldn't do it. I kept thinking of how it would effect my sister and my mother. I contemplated taking pills or getting a razor-blade but instead I just cried and cried and cried.

Eventually I went home. The crying seemed to have helped somewhat and I felt a little better. And yet I didn't tell anyone where I was at. I had learned at boarding school not to show weakness so kept a lid on what I was feeling.

Time passed but the commute became too much for me. No one spoke on the journey and then every morning I would walk across Waterloo Bridge. I became part of a human lemming trail across the bridge. At one time I stopped in the middle of the bridge and just watched people. They were rushing, they seemed asleep. I decided that I just couldn't do "London" any more

One day I was sat in the office and one of my colleagues asked me what the weather was like. My department was only 6 or 7 people in a huge open plan office of probably 100 plus people. To the window on my right was the view of a wall. To the window on my left was also the view of a wall. To the window in front of me was the view of another building 10 metres away. And to the window behind me were offices so I couldn't see through the blinds. "I don't know," I honestly replied.

My colleague went outside and came back to say that it was a beautiful sunny day, but I had absolutely no idea of that. I decided then and there that it was time to leave this job and leave London for good. I handed in my notice and within a few weeks my 4 years stay in London was over. What next?

Recap for Holiday Stress & Time Off

The above are tips to having a good holiday, a stress free holiday. But remember some stress is okay – the thrill of skydiving, or scuba diving, sailing or windsurfing.

Remember the following points:

- **Have regular time off** – don't just leave it to having a holiday once a year – have weekends away as well.
- **Have a few days after your holiday to acclimatise** – do this and you will truly enjoy your holiday more. You will be able to savour the experiences.
- **If you go abroad be aware of others customs and habits** – try not to get stressed because other customs are not doing it your way. Relax and learn a new way of being – maybe it's a way of reducing your stress.
- **Have time to rest on holiday** – spend time unwinding and relaxing before you go gallivanting around the location of your choice.
- **Have time on your own** – make time for yourself so you are able to feed yourself. Remember, only when you are truly overflowing can you give to others.
- **Nourish yourself on holiday** – take the time to stop. You are on holiday remember.
- **How to deal with Xmas and family gatherings**: keep your stress management practise going, have compassion for your family and don't get drawn in by their issues and worries and you do this by doing the breathing techniques taught in this book

Chapter Six – Questions

1. When did you last have a break where you relaxed and did nothing? What day can you schedule to have time for yourself? Organize it now. Put it in your diary.

2. Why is having time on your own and for yourself so important?

3. What things have you learned in this chapter for dealing with stressful family situations?

CHAPTER 7

The Challenges of Intimate Relationships & How To Help Let Them Thrive

During my stay in the monastery we would have visiting monks from other monasteries from around the world. One such visitor was a German monk called Venerable Nyanabodhi who had trained with the meditation teacher Ayya Khema and now lived in the monastery associated with her teachings.

After an evening meditation and chanting where locals from the towns and villages around our monastery came to join us I was speaking with Venerable Nyanabodhi. What I understood was that he had a lot of respect for the householder as he felt that to practise in a monastery with the discipline and routine was a lot easier than to practise at home with kids, partners and work. He felt that the life of a householder required a lot of patience and he respected this. At the time this surprised me, especially as I was having a hard time of it in the monastery and wanted to tell him, that personally I found it much easier in lay life!

On reflection now, I see that, yes, practise (being mindful, gentle) as a householder requires discipline. This practise in relationship is a challenge. It is a differing nature to the challenge of being in a monastic setting, but still I now understand the challenges of being in a relationship and what Venerable Nyanabodhi was talking about. It is a path that deserves respect.

But the question is, do we give ourselves the respect we are due for how we cope in our relationships? And that can be relationships of all kinds – family, spouse, children, colleagues and so on.

I have now been married 5 years and see that in relationship we are offered the opportunity to grow. Indeed your partner is a reflection of you. And very much in your face so to speak. They are there all the time. The wonderful things about them, are a reflection of you; the not so nice things about them are, also, a reflection of you. They are one of our greatest teachers – they really are. And when you start to see that they are a reflection of you and rather than trying to change them, you start to change yourself – well, a whole new world opens up. A world of connection, love, joy and bliss. It does. We want for the others to change, but that is not our role. We cannot change anyone else. We can only change ourselves. And our close relationships show us exactly where we need to change.

So in hindsight, I agree wholeheartedly with Venerable Nyanabodhi if I've understood him correctly – that to practise Buddhism, or mindfulness or meditation in a household, with a spouse, and children deserves respect. This chapter offers you some tools around relationships to give you the support so that you can get the most out of these relationships and grow as a person.

Relationships are a powerful tool for growth, and the following chapter will offer you some tools to start to see it this way again. Primarily, this chapter looks at the relationships you have with your partners, lovers, husbands or wives but the tools and techniques can be transferred to all relationships – from work colleagues to family, from friends to children.

57. Investing In Your Relationship

Imagine you have a bank account. All year you put no money in it, you pay no attention to it and you forget it exists. At the end of the year, what do you have in return? Nothing.

If on the other hand you make deposits on a weekly basis, and put any spare cash in as savings what do you get at the end of the year? Yes, a healthy bank account. The same goes for our personal relationships. Put nothing in, you get nothing out. Take your relationship for granted and they take you for granted.

But if on the other hand you invest time with your partner doing things you love doing on a regular basis, what happens? If you praise and nourish your partner and are compassionate when things are not going so well what do you get in return? Yes, a thriving and healthy relationship.

Sometimes we get stuck in everyday life and lose sight of what the most important things are for ourselves – like our health or our loved ones. And it is only when they are taken away from us – through separation, or illness that we take note. We can see people around us who have lost loved ones through separation who pine for what could have been. And yet a question we could ask is did they truly nourish this relationship? Did they fill the bank, so to speak, on a regular basis? Or did they take the relationship for granted and now that it has gone they realise exactly what they had?

And how does this relate to you? Do you take your loved one for granted? Have you done that in the past? The world turns with such ferocity nowadays – there is so much to do, activities to fill our days with that we have less and less time for our loved ones. And therefore we have less and less credit in our "relationship bank". How about you start investing again? How about you start to spend time with your wife or husband rather than on Facebook? How about taking your loved one for a meal out rather than sitting and watching the TV?

When you start to give to your relationship well it overflows into other areas of your life – you become energized, alive, passionate, juicy, interested in life. Sure it is easier to plop down in front of the TV, but when you switch it off and go and make love instead, you both feel great and you both feel connected.

So what are some of the things you can do to fill your "relationship bank" up?

- Giving wonderful comments
- Buying flowers for your loved one
- Taking them on a surprise date
- Going on a relaxed weekend break
- Having one evening a week where your sole focus is on each other, no children, TV, Facebook and so on.
- Kiss and caress your loved one every time you see them
- Hold their face in your hands, look directly in their eyes and tell them you love them. (This tip came from my wife who says that women melt when you do this sincerely.)

And what happens when you do this? What happens when you fill the "relationship bank" up? Well, it starts to pay dividends – you get on wonderfully well with your loved one, it is pure pleasure being with them, you feel like you are growing closer together, your love and respect grows for them, and they give to you unconditionally. The things that "were" a problem seem to disappear. They are no longer important.

Do what you can do today to nourish and fill your relationship.

58. Being Grateful For What You Have

We have covered this point before about gratitude and we cover it again here because of its pure importance. That which we focus on grows. And most of us in the West have been deftly trained to focus on that which is not working. So what grows? Exactly – that which is not working.

So in your relationship you get that which you focus on. Having gratitude for your loved ones and your family helps you to bring that focus into a positive slant. What am I grateful for with my partner, wife or husband? So often in life we take for granted that which is most important to us. We take it as a given that our loved ones are the way they are but we never acknowledge the positive aspects – we take them for granted. But those things that we take for granted the most are the things we would miss the most if they were not there e.g. your body, your eyes, your health, your partner, your children.

And again it is often only when these things are taken away from you do you truly appreciate and feel grateful for what you have. But sometimes it is too late by then.

So the following exercise is great for starting to appreciate and love what you have in your life at this time. Not in the future and not in the past. Now. Here. Right here now. This minute.

EXERCISE 35

Being Grateful For Your Partner

1. Find your stress management journal. And write in it a list of everything you appreciate about your spouse, lover, or partner (you can put in family member or anyone else you are close to).

2. Write a list of everything they do which you are grateful for. What is wonderful? What is great? What would you miss if they were to go? What would you feel like if they were to go and what do you appreciate the most in them?

3. This could be: they are strong and fit, they are healthy, they have a wonderfully open heart, they are so kind, they are wonderful lovers, they don't get angry at me when I am not being nice, they are brilliant cooks, they clean up after me, they always say nice things to me, they listen to what I say, they are clean, they are so generous with their time, they are so spiritual, they are so focussed, they put up with so much from me, they are so patient...

4. This list could go on and on but write something down.

5. And once you have written this list down really feel the feeling in your heart, and in your body of how grateful you are. Feel this feeling. And this is so important – the most important point. It so it is so important that you feel this gratitude flowing from your heart.

6. And when the feeling has reached its most powerful about how amazing your partner is and how grateful you are for them press your thumb and second fingertips together for 10 seconds.

7. And if you notice negative qualities coming up, keep coming back to the positive. Remember you have to reprogram your mind to the positive now. So every time a negative thought or something you don't like about them comes up, come back to the positive, come back to what you appreciate in them and press your 2nd finger and thumb together. Feel the good feelings coming back to you.

Be grateful for all that you have and you will find that your partner will blossom – for you see all the beauty in them rather than criticising them all the time.

The saying:

"We are what we think about"

Rings true here as much as anywhere. For when you are focusing on all that you appreciate in your partner then what you notice about them will be more things to appreciate within them. They will still be doing the things which annoyed you before but because you have started to program yourself to see the good, you either won't notice the other things or won't be around when they do it.

59. Compliment Your Partner From Your Heart

Now you have your list with all the wonderful qualities of your partner (and keep adding to this list) start to use it.

How much do you like receiving compliments? How does it make you feel? Do you feel good?

Some people love receiving compliments and some people struggle with hearing people say good things about them. They feel uncomfortable with hearing nice things about themselves because they have been taught to be tough on themselves. But over time the more we compliment people about something specific the easier it can be to hear. And you now have a list of wonderful things that you appreciate in your partner from the previous exercise so you can now tell them what you appreciate in them.

What is important with this exercise is that you come from a space in your heart which is full. If you are really angry or stressed – this will not come across so well – it might not come across at all. Still your mind and heart with a couple of deep breaths and a walk and then tell them.

Tell them from your heart what a wonderful being they are.

And to start off with they might be shocked at this but that's okay. Keep giving.

Mother Theresa once said,

"If you are kind, people may accuse you of selfish motives. Be kind anyway."

There is a story related by Ajahn Brahm, a senior monk in the Thai Forest tradition, which goes along the following lines. He was based in Western Australia and part of his remit as a monk was to go and teach meditation to the local prisoners. He was teaching some of the basic principles of Buddhism when one of the prisoners said that there was one guard who was really nasty. The prisoner had to serve tea to him everyday and he said he never smiled, or said hello and was just gruff and rude to him.

Ajahn Brahm suggested that the prisoner show loving kindness to this guard, which means to open your heart towards someone. So everyday with his cup of tea, the prisoner said hello to this guard. And everyday the guard either ignored him or continued in his previous manner. But after 6 months, there was a huge shift. The prisoner kept saying hello and sending this love to this guard and one day the guard turned to prisoner and said hello back. He replied. He responded respectfully. This guard, who was the most feared in the prison, had said hello.

And what this story shows is that no matter how tough or unresponsive your partner is to your appreciations, eventually you will melt their heart and melt yours in the process. You are a powerful being. What type of relationship do you want?

60. Seeing The Positive Rather Than The Negative

The Western mind has a tendency to get lost in the negative. Watch your internal dialogue when you are washing up or cleaning or doing some task which doesn't require much concentration. Do you start to get lost in the negative – "What has she done here? Why is he so messy? What have I done to deserve this?"

And what happens is that we create a state of anxiety from a situation where no problem existed. Suddenly we are in a rage and don't know why.

So the trick is to watch your mind. Watch it go into the negative and don't go there. Stay on the positive. Repeat affirmations to yourself, "I am happy and content", "I am coping", "I am calm and relaxed". And every time you get distracted come back to the affirmations.

One of the things that happens with relationships is that we start to take our partners for granted as has been mentioned before. And because of our tendency to fall into the negative we only see what they haven't done well.

Imagine what it's like for the partner, always being criticised and never receiving any praise? Could you imagine that they will shut down, not want to listen to anything their partner (you) wants to say.

So don't get lost in the negative. Focus on the positive. Use the list that you have written for what you are grateful for and focus on this. Because what happens is that if you focus on the negative you will get more of it.

Focus on the positive and you will get more positive. When you are starting to go off on one at something they have done keep coming back to this list of the things you do appreciate or coming back to what you do want. Change how you feel – we will talk about this over and over again because it is so important.

It doesn't mean that you let your partner get away with everything (we will talk about communication later on in this chapter) but you focus on what they are doing well rather than what they are always failing at.

Ask yourself this: How does it make you feel to be complimented and praised continually? How does it make you feel to be criticised and shouted at continually? You can probably feel it in you as you read this. You know which one you prefer so give others that beauty as well.

61. Making Time For Yourself (Become Your Own Partner)

One thing that most people find challenging in a relationship is finding time for themselves. It is almost like the relationship becomes one person instead of two people. Everything is done together and sometimes you can lose a sense of who you truly are.

And what this can evoke and cause is frustration. If you have a more dominant partner then you might find that you are going along with their decisions rather than going along with what you feel deep inside.

So it is important that both of you make time so you can be on your own. This means doing things without your partner. I personally recommend doing things where you are on your own completely: going for a walk, going to the gym, going to a church or a meditation hall. A place where you can settle yourself and find calm within.

By taking this time out to find yourself and to balance yourself you then take that energy and feeling back into the relationship. When you fill yourself up then you can give to others. If you are empty then you have nothing to give to others.

Usually when partners have had conflict and have a period of a few days apart they feel so much better about each other. When they see each other again they are happy and contented – they are balanced. But why wait for a conflict to arise before you spend time on your own? Schedule it in so that the conflict doesn't arise.

So find time for a couple of hours a week where you do your own thing: sit in your room on your own reading, or writing. Go for a walk on your own, study something uplifting.

Your partner might not understand at the beginning why you need time away from each other because they are not used to it. But that is okay. It is important to carry through with it all the same. The benefits you will receive and therefore conversely your partner will receive will be huge. And after a few weeks of seeing how happy and balanced you are for this time your partner will then have less resistance to it.

62. Making Time For Both of You

And just as important as making time for yourself is the importance of making time for both of you.

Again, we go through life, filling our days up with things. But most of these things are unimportant – watching TV, or surfing the net. And the things which are important get ignored: spending time with our families, spending time with ourselves.

So sit down with your partner and block off a time each week where you spend quality time together doing something for yourselves rather for someone else.

This could be: walking together, visiting a beautiful gallery, going to a restaurant together, cooking each other a candle lit dinner, making love – making your love life come alive again, stepping out of your comfort zone, painting or creating something together.

I personally wouldn't recommend watching TV or going shopping together because TV requires no connection to each other – it shuts the mind down and going shopping can be very stressful and isn't really that romantic – women generally enjoy shopping whereas men generally don't.

So find things that you both love. And again you get back what you are prepared to put in. If you work hard at anything with an open heart the rewards can be huge.

63. How To Communicate Well – Talking Stick/ Use Of Language

Communication in a relationship is so important to the well being of both parties. If the communication is poor then there is more chance of conflict arising.

But most of us are not taught how to communicate properly – we learn from our families and from TV (good communication doesn't sell so well on TV or have such high ratings).

In my own upbringing there was a lot of anger and shouting when people were communicating about delicate subjects. So I vowed from a very young age that I wouldn't argue – and I found that I couldn't really argue – I just used to see red and my mind would go blank.

But this used to cause me huge problems. I didn't know how to get my point across so I would either ignore it and get more angry because of this, or blame everything on the other person. And to be honest neither of those worked at all.

So through time and watching experts of communication at work, I started to understand some key points about communicating with partners:

64. Stop Using "You" In A Blaming Way

I have found that many people when communicating with partners or others use the blaming technique. This technique alienates the other person because they feel that they are being blamed for something that they don't agree with.
What is meant by this? When you are talking to a spouse or partner it is important that you don't use the language of attack:

"You always hurt me"
"You're always messy"
"You always say such nasty things"

When you come from this perspective it is like you are attacking the other person – you are making a judgement about them. And they can either agree or not. It is like you are stating a fact. You are like this.

And what this creates is conflict. This conflict is how most of us communicate.

What is a better way of communicating? When you come from your perspective – saying how you feel about the situation then this less offensive and less attacking. Obviously some people will still find this unpleasant because you are speaking the truth but it takes the edge off communication.

Ways of saying this are:

"I feel hurt when you tell me that you don't like that part of me."
"I am tired of cleaning up after you. Please clean up after yourself."
"I feel let down and disappointed when you don't turn up to meet me on time."

By saying how you feel you change the perspective – it is not about blaming the other person but how you perceive the situation. The energy you give out is less attacking.

Words are very important in communicating with others but it is only part of the equation. If you only change your words then things will get a little better but it is not the only thing which needs to change if you want to have amazing communication.

65. Speak From A Calm And Assertive Place

If you come from a really angry place when you communicate, well you are likely to get a similar response in reply. Even if your words are absolutely wonderful, if they come from a horrible place, then they will not come across in the way that we want them to – to heal.

Watch people in social situations when they communicate. If people are angry and aggressive, they attract that out of others. If people are kind and gentle then, again, they attract that in return.

So the key to this point is that if you are aware that you are angry and saying something from this place is likely to start an argument – don't say it. I repeat – don't say it. Say nothing – leave the room, go for a walk. When you say it from this place the other person will feel attacked and attack you right back, an argument ensues and both of you have a horrible time.

The teacher Esther Hicks says that before getting into a fight, pull the fists back. Before getting into an argument, pull the words back. And before getting into a negative mental space, pull the thoughts back.

Indeed, do you ever feel that you have to say something? You see something happening which really annoys you and you have to say something. Well, you know what I am going to say. Don't say anything. Not then, maybe later when you have calmed down.

Have you ever seen people on a bus saying something to kids or noisy people? They usually come from an angry place, "You shouldn't be doing this!" and therefore they get an angry response and wonder why. They blame the kids but in fact they are just getting a reflection of their own anger.

So before you say something to a loved one, come from a calm and assertive place. How do you do this?

EXERCISE 36

Communicating From A Calm And Assertive Place

Before you communicate, do this exercise. If you don't have time to do it, be aware that you might get a unpleasant reaction to what you say.

1. Focus your attention on your stomach (you don't need to look at your stomach but focus your mind on the feeling and sensations in your stomach). Place your hands there.

2. Breathe in for a count of 4 while focusing your attention on your stomach.

3. Hold your breath for a count of 4, while again focusing on your stomach.

4. Breathe out for a count of 4 with your attention still locked on your stomach.

5. Keep this breathing going for 5 repetitions. Then stop for 30 seconds. If you feel more balanced go and speak what you need to say. If not keep repeating until you feel more balanced.

You can do this exercise for any reason but doing it before communicating makes such a difference. Things you say are heard rather than shot back at you in anger.

66. Using a Talking Stick

A talking stick is a communication tool which has been around for a long, long time. It is a tool which I first came across when studying Native American traditions. I have found it invaluable in dealing with challenging situations.

The idea of a talking stick is that whoever is holding this stick holds the conversation. This means that no one else can interrupt when this person is speaking.

The idea though is that it is done in an empowering way rather than a dictatorial way, for example, once you have the stick you don't then start to have a go at everyone, blaming, being rude and nasty. No, the idea of a talking stick is to allow the person holding it to speak from the heart, and for the other person listening, to hear what that person's heart has to say.

When we are in conversation with people, often times we are in our world relating to what that person is saying through our own experiences. This means that in a lot of cases we do not truly hear what the other person is saying.

What a talking stick does is gives the space for people to speak and to hear.

This tool is especially good in families with teenage children. As adults we sometimes don't see that our children are growing up and therefore give them little space to think for themselves. A talking stick gives children the space and the power to speak about what they are feeling and not to feel like they are being dis-empowered.

There are three different ways of using a talking stick.

1. The first and most common is: The person who is holding the stick speaks. They speak from the heart using language like, "I feel…, I think…, I am…, I need…, I want… etc. They stay away from blaming the other person but speak from their own perspective of how a situation makes them feel.

The first person speaks for about 5 minutes or so before handing the stick over to their partner (the partner replies to what you have said so it is important that you don't cover too many points).

The other person listens and does not interrupt, even if they feel the urge to. It is probably this urge which has caused the need for a talking stick. Do you really listen to your partner from your heart?

Once the first person is finished the stick is then passed onto the partner who has their turn to speak. Remember to come from the heart at all times.

Don't ask questions of the other person all the time as they won't be able to answer.

Also be aware that the other person can only reply to so much so don't talk for too long.

---

2. The second method is for when one person really doesn't feel heard. They feel that their partner doesn't hear them and that they need to be heard in order for the relationship to continue.

The first person who is holding the stick speaks and follows the same principles from the first example.

When they have finished speaking they pass the stick onto their partner. Instead of replying the partner will repeat back what they have understood from their partner.

Once the partner has repeated back what they understood they pass the stick back to the first person. The first person will say whether they were understood properly or not. If not they repeat again what they meant.

This passing back of the stick continues until the first person feels that they have been properly understood.

To start off with it is likely that this will go on for a little while, but what this teaches is the art of heart to heart communication. It teaches you to both speak and listen from the heart. It also teaches the person who is listening to actually listen – to pay attention.

Once the first person feels that they have been heard they then pass the stick onto the second person and the second person has their opportunity to reply. It is then up to the first person to repeat back what they have understood.

What you will find is that the first person has as much difficulty in hearing their partner as they feel their partner has in hearing them. Often times what annoys us the most in others is what we do the most ourselves.

This is a tremendously eye opening tool and can change the way you relate to each other in an instant. No longer are you coming from different places. You both suddenly hear and understand each other.

But as with any practise, it takes practise so be patient with yourself and your partner.

---

3. The third form of talking stick is as part 2 or part 1 but communication has really broken down and trust is no longer there. A third person is brought in to hold the space. This means that if one person keeps interrupting the other then this third party steps in.

This is obviously a last resort but it can also be the wake up call you both need to open your hearts again and look at the joy in the relationship rather than the anger or sadness.

EXERCISE 37

Making a Talking Stick To Use For Better Communication

A talking stick itself is a piece of wood maybe 30 – 40 centimetres long and 3 to 4 centimetres in diameter.

1. As you are using this tool for the relationship it is really good to have both of you go out into the woods together. Make an afternoon of it and go for a walk.

2. Set an intent before you step into the woods that you are looking for a stick to bring heart to heart communication into your relationship. Ask to be drawn to a stick that you can take home.

3. When you do find a stick which jumps out at you, ask if you can take it. We have got used to taking without asking for things in the West so this is good practise for learning how to ask. If it is your stick you will know inside if the answer is yes or not.

4. Make the stick into something sacred and creative. Maybe tie a feather to it, put some crystals in the stick or design some markings on it. Make it special – it has a very special purpose – that of bringing beauty into the world and into your own life…

5. Do a little ceremony together. Light a candle or have a fire and take it in turns to set your intent with the stick. What do you want to get from it: a closer relationship, heart to heart communication, more wisdom, more fun and joy?

6. When you are finished you are then ready to use the stick.

The above tools are some of the ways to improve communication between you and your partner.

But the secret? Don't take it or yourself too seriously, tickle each other, have fun, let go of trying to hold everything together. You are doing so magnificently well! Well done!

67. Receiving Yourself And Your Partner

This concept comes up a lot in this book: receiving yourself and your partner.

A lot of people in the West have a tendency to be very hard on themselves. They are never quite happy with themselves or with the people that they are with – they gossip, put others down and don't feel so good about themselves.

But a key to a successful and relatively stress free relationship is allowing yourself to let go of trying to be perfect all the time. It is letting go of trying to get things right and be something that you are not.

We have such pressure on ourselves as humans to be like the Joneses; to be like the image of the film stars and sports heroes. But we are not like them. We are like ourselves. And the sooner we realise that we are truly beautiful for who we are now, the sooner we step into a place, a magnificent beauty: a place where we love ourselves despite the mistakes, the pimples and the wrinkles. We love ourselves because of who we are.

And the truth is that only when you truly start to receive yourself as you are can you ever expect to truly receive anyone else. And another amazing thing is that only by receiving yourself as you are now will you ever be happy with anything in the future. I think it's worth it if you ask me.

So how do you receive your partner? In the same way. Once you have received yourself – accepted yourself for all the mistakes you've made, either blamed yourself for or not forgiven yourself for, then you can open your heart to them.

You forgive your partner for not being quite enough. You forgive them for not living up to your standards – which you will probably realise that no one ever has and probably no one ever will! You let go of trying to mould them into being how you want them to be. And you will see that, once you have received yourself that you can let go of trying to control them because you have let go of trying to control yourself.

EXERCISE 38

Receiving Yourself and Your Partner

1. Place your hand over your heart. Imagine that you have a mouth in the centre of your chest. Imagine that when you breathe in you are breathing in and out of your heart rather than from your mouth or nose.

2. Feel the gentle breath going in and out, filling your heart with oxygen. You feel relaxed and calm. Settle yourself into you – feel your body relaxing, your muscles releasing any tension and your mind becoming still.

3. Start to repeat these words either out loud or under your breath:

   "I receive myself as I am today"
   "I receive myself for who I am"
   "I forgive myself for anything that I did in the past.
   This was past and I have learned from this. I can forgive myself now."
   "I live in the present now – and I am joyful as I breathe in and out."
   "I forgive my partner for anything they may have said or done."
   "I let go of the past and live in the wonderment of now."
   "I receive my partner for who they are and let go of trying to change them."
   "I receive myself and all those around me."

When you have finished repeating these words close your eyes.

Stop.
Feel.
Breathe in through your heart…
Breathe out through your heart…
Breathe in… Receive yourself and others…
Breathe out… Let go of trying to change others…
Everything is working out perfectly.
Relax, be calm, be still. You are magnificent.

You can change the above exercise into a script and record it onto an MP3 player or onto your computer. Personalise it so that you are hearing, "I receive myself and others."

By listening to it you can help to speed the process along because you can listen to this at any time of the day, in any place.

68. Be Patient With Your Partner

Being patient with your partner makes a lot of sense, but how often do we in the West throw being patient out the window? How often do you shout, or say things out of place rather than taking a deep breath and cultivating patience? In a society where we go for instant meals and quicker, better, best, patience is rarely a cultivated internal quality. And yet in relationships it is the difference between cultivating a deep and meaningful connection with another soul or finding no depth at all.

Life is not always smiley and happy – you wouldn't want it that way either – you would get bored. Life has its challenges and so do relationships. You learn patience during these times. Indeed, one of the monks said to me one day that the only way you can learn patience is when things are not going "your" way. When someone is annoying you, or a situation is challenging, he said, this is the best time to cultivate patience. He said that it is really difficult to learn patience when everything is going the way you want it.

And this is so true in relationships. Sometimes things aren't going quite the way you want it. And sometimes your partner or friends really annoy you. What this teaching speaks of is that when things are challenging this is when you learn patience.

I have personally found in my own life that it has not been when things have been going smoothly that I learn the most. The reason that I have been able to write this book is because things have been very challenging in my life and I have learned from them. I have learned things like patience when things seemed to be falling apart around me.

EXERCISE 39

Learning To Be Patient With Your Loved Ones

This exercise is to be used when you are feeling annoyed or challenged by your partner or loved ones. Maybe you want to react and get angry at them. Before you say anything read through and practice this exercise.

There is a well known saying I learned in the monastery:

"This too will pass."

It stems from and has been adapted to a Buddhist teaching that says whatever is happening in your life it will change. It is based around the teachings of impermanence ("anicca" in Pali – pronounced anni-cha) which states that everything in the universe is impermanent, everything changes. The idea with this exercise is that you apply this saying to whatever comes up in your life.

1. You feel annoyed with your partner or something is coming up in your life. Acknowledge where you are while adding the phrase, "this too will pass". For example:

   "I feel terrible – this too will pass" (feel the feeling, acknowledge it)
   "I am so excited – this too will pass"
   "I am so annoyed by her/him – this too will pass"
   "I feel so depressed by this situation – this too will pass"

2. Say this out loud or in your head. And when you say it – make a reflection – how did you feel yesterday – did you feel the same? And if you did, go back to a time when you did feel different.

3. Whatever you are feeling be aware that it will change. If you feel great acknowledge it, but also be aware that it will change. The only thing which is constant in this universe is change.

4. Breathe deeply and relax.

This is such a beautiful teaching as it allows you to relax into the moment. It allows you to be just who you are now and takes the energy out of how you are feeling.

What this technique teaches is not only patience but also letting go of getting attached to the good and the bad. What it means is that you don't get lost in over indulging in the pleasure and you don't get lost over indulging in the pain. And sometimes we do do that. We go into self-pity and become the victim when things get difficult whereas if we let go of it – it just is e.g. I have a pain in my leg full stop. The story stops there, "I have a pain."When you do this the weight is lifted from your shoulders.

But it doesn't mean that you don't enjoy life – oh no, not at all, instead you can really enjoy and thrive in life:

"Life is the journey, not the destination."

So see that when things are not going well with your partner or in your life that this is the time to learn patience, this is the time to master yourself. And when you find the light in everything that happens in your life, well, that is when you start to move towards, en-light-enment.

69. Your Partner is a Reflection of You

Relationships are a great and powerful teacher. Here we have in front of us a person to show us our shining and also where we are stuck. When you start to see that your partner is a reflection of you a new level of growth can be achieved.

As a society we pay huge amounts every year on therapists and counsellors to tell us where we are stuck, and yet here we have in front of us, in our partners, a wonderful mirror to show us the same thing. I wholeheartedly support the use of therapists and counsellors because of their amazing ability to shift us, and yet I believe that in our partners we have another way of growing.

We are attracted to people who are reflections of us. We are attracted to people who have similar core values as us. The patterns that annoy you about your partner or your loved ones are the same patterns that you have. For example, it annoys you that your partner doesn't tidy up her clothes and yet although you tidy your clothes you leave your office in a mess. But because you are always in your office – you don't notice it. The fact that it really annoys you can show you where you are stuck as in this case. It is not easy to hear. That is why we pay the therapists – to tell us these things. As Jung stated, "until you make the unconscious conscious, it will direct your life and you will call it fate."

When you start to acknowledge that this is the case you can start to see that your partner is your greatest teacher. They are showing you where you are stuck. If your partner flies off the handle all the time – this is showing what you do, not necessarily with them but maybe with others or with yourself. So now you see your pattern, you can start to change – in this example you can start to have more patience with others as you can feel what it is like to be on the receiving end of this anger.

This also works on the positive side as well. For all the wonderful qualities you see in your partner, you have in yourself too. When you are having trouble seeing the light in yourself just see it being reflected back by your partner.

What wonderful teachers are partners are! So rejoice in all the wonderment that is in your life.

When things are not going so well with your partner or you are having a rough time in your life and are having trouble seeing much good in what you or others do, please do the following exercise:

EXERCISE 40

Seeing The Reflection of You In Your Partner

1. Get your journal out and write down the things that annoy you about your partner (if you don't have a partner do it for people that are closest to you – family/ friends). Once you have your list change it from 3rd person to 1st person e.g. They/ she/ he does this....to I do this....

2. For example, she's really angry to I'm really angry. He's really messy to I'm really messy. By doing this you are taking the sting out of the energy that you are aiming at your partner, or family member. It's not about giving yourself a hard time again. It is just allowing it to be. You are not perfect, but neither are your loved ones. When you start to let them be the way they are and love them all the same your relationship reaches a whole new level.

3. Then do it for the positive. What are the positive qualities? Do the same again, changing 3rd person to 1st person. For example, she is really loving to I am really loving. (If it doesn't resonate with you, remember that your partner is a reflection of you – you might not be able to see it or resonate with it, but as Jung said, if it is turning up in your life then somehow it relates to you. By acknowledging it you can start to let it go.

The idea of this exercise is to start to take ownership for who you are and how you feel – again receiving yourself for who you are and it helps to open your heart to compassion. When you realise you are angry you can do something about it.

70. Keeping Your Heart Open

This is one of the main things that I have learned from my own partner. And it is that no matter what is happening try to remain in the heart. I spoke about this in the exercise on receiving yourself and your partner. I spoke about imagining a mouth in the centre of your chest and breathing into your heart which comes from the HeartMath Institute. Well, try to keep this space when things start to go wobbly – if not we create a lot of scenarios in our minds which aren't true.

Visualise and feel, how do you want your relationship to be? And then focus on that. No matter what is going on keep your attention on this highest vision of how you see your relationship to be. This can mean visualising images you have of your relationship when it was working really well or keep drawing on and remembering happy times. Give as little attention and focus to challenging times – for "this too will pass." It always does, but when you kick up a fuss and a stink rather than staying in your heart you create more to fuss and worry about. Be gentle and focus on the love that you have felt in your relationship.

71. Keeping Lines of Communication Open.

When things are challenging, or we think they are challenging we can actually create a situation which we thought existed but in reality doesn't exist in the other person's mind.

It is as if we create our own misfortune.

I used to find in the monastery that when I had to speak to someone about something that I didn't like it could create tension. The other person could feel hurt and I found that problems could arise between us if I didn't engage with the person straight afterwards.

I remember one example in the monastery with one of the kitchen managers. I had disagreed with something he had said and told him so. I think he felt quite upset. But as we were sat at breakfast a few minutes later I started to ask him about something completely different – taking interest in him.

It shifted the energy and our relationship returned to normal – we didn't talk about what had happened as that was over. But by speaking as if nothing has happened you return the relationship to normal. This doesn't mean denying it, it means it is spoken and then it is dropped.

You have said what was needed and you are now moving on. This is especially good for children – you tell them what is not okay but then you drop it – you don't hold it against them, you forgive them.

But, as in the above example with the kitchen manager, if I hadn't done this – especially in a community where we were all living so close to each other – well it could have caused friction. And I can tell you that I learned the hard way with this one and it took many years of practise.

So in applying this to your own life, if you have had an argument or you feel things aren't going well. Be patient. Be kind. Talk to your partner, not necessarily about what is not working but about anything. Clear the air – step into a place which can be frightening but which heals so many upsets. Keep focusing on the light and don't hold onto things – the air will clear, it always does.

72. What Energy and "Vibes" Am I Giving Out

In a relationship, any for that matter, be it at work or with your partner, it is so important to be aware of what you are giving out.

What does this mean? Well, you have just got back from a long day at work and your partner has cooked a really lovely meal. Your partner has spent time and effort trying to make you feel good.

But you are really tired and don't really notice what your partner has prepared – you are still lost in your day. You are also quite short with your partner. Your partner gets upset and you have an argument. And you are wondering what you have done to deserve this.

In this instance you have created this scenario by the energy you are giving out. By coming home angry and still preoccupied with work you bring that energy into the home. And therefore when you communicate with your partner this is the energy they pick up – that you are angry and this is what they react to – they don't know if you are angry at them but whatever it is they are on the end of it.

So it is very important to be aware of where you are at. If you are feeling angry then be aware of what you say to your partner or to anyone for that matter. It is your responsibility to deal with what you are feeling and when you do this – it is amazing – your relationships are revolutionized. You think before you speak and are aware of what energy you are giving out.

EXERCISE 41

Learning Communication From Others

1. Think of someone really peaceful and calm that you know and think of them now (if you can't think of anyone think of a public figure like The Dalai Lama or Nelson Mandela.) You can write this down in your journal as well. How do you interact with them? Do you get angry with them? Probably not as the energy they are giving out is calm and balanced. (If this is not someone you have met then imagine how you would be around them).

2. Now think of someone in your life who is always stressed and chaotic. How do you feel around them? Do you feel good or chaotic and stressed when you are around them? Again I presume that you are likely to feel pretty stressed being around them.

3. Now look at yourself. How do you think people feel around you? Would you want to be around someone like you? Realise that when you are stressed and chaotic others probably feel just as stressed.

4. Notice this. Acknowledge that you have the power to change this. You are in complete control. And when you are feeling stressed and chaotic. Stop. Practise some of the techniques in this book – the meditation, the compassion, the counting to 10, and the energy you give out will be so much different.

5. And the result? Your life will be less stressed. And so will the people around you.

73. How To Stop Arguments

Arguments can be a waste of energy. They trigger unpleasant emotions in the other person and unpleasant emotions in yourself. When we start getting angry and start arguing we use language and say things that we wouldn't usually say.

And what happens is that this causes the other person to react in a similar manner. This keeps escalating until one person feels like they are the winner.

To be truthful, there is very little wisdom in an argument – most of the things we can say when we are arguing come from the inner wounded child. And therefore this can trigger the inner wounded child in the other person and a full blown argument can ensue.

So what is the advice about arguing?

The first thing is to take responsibility for what you feel. That is the first thing. If you are feeling angry, you project anger out. And when you speak angry words then you are likely to get angry responses.

When you take responsibility for what you feel, you then realise that if you are to say something in this volatile state, you are likely to cause a volatile situation. It is therefore your responsibility to go out of the room, go for a walk, go to the gym. Deal with the anger that is coming up. Deal with it yourself and don't dump it onto the other person.

Think about it. How do you feel when someone really comes at you with aggression or anger? Do you either retreat but later on explode and harbour anger about this person for years afterwards or do you attack back?

And how do you feel when someone comes at you from the heart? "I feel really upset at what you said." They come at you from a caring place, with a gentle but firm energy, using a calm and balanced voice. Sure it might be hard to hear but this is what heart to heart communication is about. Speaking and coming from the heart. And in this scenario you might well stop in your tracks and become aware of where you are at.

My partner was telling me a story last night. She said that some people she knew were maltreating some animals. It really upset her and triggered something deep within. She was really angry.

So what did she do? For three days and three nights she dealt with her anger. For she knew that if she confronted the said individuals from a place of anger there could be a huge explosion.

So she paced and worked on herself – breathing, walking, balancing – a lot of the techniques that are taught throughout this book – until she was ready. She knew she was ready when she felt that she had dealt with "her" anger. She did her part of the deal. It was her responsibility to deal with her anger.

So after 3 days and nights she confronted these people. She spoke from her heart and told them what she felt. Now this did trigger aggression in the other person but because she had come from the heart and she just felt this love emanating from her heart, they withdrew really quickly.

This story shows that it is up to you to deal with your emotions before you speak to your loved ones and partners. And this in itself helps to stop arguments.

If the other person confronts you – then you don't have to engage – you are responsible for yourself remember. Why engage in something that makes you feel awful? Remember to use the exercise of Tonglen (P. 38) which I teach in this book.

The solution to this is to talk and resolve things when you are both balanced and calm. Sit down and talk. And make sure that both of you have open hearts. Try using a talking stick – this I have found is an invaluable tool.

EXERCISE 42

Healing the Relationship – What To Do When Things Are Challenging

Take your stress management journal or notebook. And ask yourself the following questions:

a. What can I do differently to help heal this situation?
b. In what ways can I act to help resolve this?
c. What am I doing to provoke this reaction in my partner?
d. In what ways can I help to heal my partner?
e. What behaviours am I using that I need to let go of now e.g. trying to control, trying to change others, flying off the handle in anger, repressing everything and not saying anything.

Write down honest answers – for you do know how to resolve any given situation in your life. That is the power that we have as humans – the ability to self-reflect, to self-heal.

But it is important in this exercise that you come from your heart about yourself. You dictate the changes in your life so focus on you and not the other person.

After the funeral of my father life seemed to go into limbo. Here I had been focusing on spending time with my father but now he was gone – a void opened up. I was still working and living on the outskirts of Guildford, south of London but now the monotonous data entry job felt too much. Here I was entering the same bits of information every 15 minutes. It had served a purpose before – allowing me to leave when I needed to go down to see my father but now it was what it was – boring.

I saw that my mother was struggling to come to terms with the death of my father – or at least this is what I wanted to see. I needed to be needed rather than face up to myself. My parents had divorced 7 years previously and it seemed that my mother felt guilty. It was as if she felt they should have stayed together.

As I was not wanting to look at my own pain I decided I needed to move back to my mother's house to lift her spirits. In hindsight, I was pretty empty at that point, my cup had almost nothing in it so how I expected to lift anyone's spirit I do not know. Indeed, I did not manage to lift anyone let alone my own self. I took jobs locally and ended up working in a hospital doing administration. The pay was low, the prospects non-existent as it was a temporary job, and during winter I worked in a room without natural light, and for days on end I would see no natural light.

As I was not letting go of my pain or dealing with any of my issues I started to spiral into depression. I started drinking more heavily and starting going off to support my local football team, Portsmouth, which required more heavy drinking. I seemed to be falling into my father's pattern – drink, but I didn't know what else to do – this is what everyone around me was doing – repression, drinking, outburst, repression, drinking... and so on. The part I seemed to miss out on was the outburst. I had learned to suppress my emotions so firmly at boarding school that it didn't matter how much I drank I still would not lose "control". Something had to change.

It was the longest I had lived in my family home since I had left for boarding school when I was 11. I felt dis-empowered, useless, a waste of space and these feelings of being crazy, depressed and suicidal started to powerfully flow over me. I couldn't go on any more and wanted to end my life. There was nothing here for me now. I started to take anti-depressants and this eased the feelings slightly. But the drugs just made me feel numb – I still wasn't dealing with the pain I was hiding deep inside.

I organized to see a psychiatrist but as the waiting list was months long I realized I would have to do something myself to change and quickly. It was touch and go whether I would make it. I had been taking anti-depressants now for 6 months but there was nothing to my life: job, football, alcohol. I had few friends and no sexual relationships. And I believed my internal dialogue that I was useless and that no one would ever love me.

I knew I had to get out from my mother's house if I was to survive. Living with my mother was driving me crazy. Again in hindsight living with her was just what

I needed to get me to a point where I would scream, "No more! I can't handle it any more!"

I asked myself what I wanted. I wanted to teach/ help others, I wanted to go somewhere warm. One night when my mother was out I started to research volunteer teaching organisations which sent people abroad. As I surfed the internet I found lots of organisations but they were all charging thousands of pounds for 3 months volunteering. I wanted to do it in exchange for the work I did.

I figured most of these companies would be based in the US – American companies were the leaders in most fields. I had a look at the first website I had visited to see where they were based. Amazingly and not so amazingly when I started to understand the laws of the universe, the company was located next to my best friend from school's house. I had walked past this building 50 times at least in the past 12 years!

This synchronicity inspired me to call the company saying what I was looking for – to volunteer without needing to pay for it. They commented how interesting it was that I contacted them at this time as there were only 2-3 such spaces available globally and one had just become available as we spoke! Again, now knowing the law of attraction, my powerful desire for change had literally moved mountains...

I was asked to send my CV through and within a month I was working at this company's head office in the south of England. I was going to be sent to Ghana at the end of April so would have time to learn the ropes. I was called into my manager's office at the end of March after being there for a few weeks. He asked me what I was doing in a week's time and I replied, "no plans". He said, "Great, we need you to go to Ghana early – you're leaving next week!" Wow, things change quickly. I spent the next week rushing round the south of England getting the jabs I needed for yellow fever and packing my bags.

My mother was sad to see me go and yet she seemed happy at the same time, glad that I was going off on an adventure. I was very excited. Is this what I need? I flew into Accra, Ghana the end of that week and a new chapter in my life started. I started work as a volunteer coordinator – accommodation, food, flights were paid for and I received a small allowance which more than covered my expenses. From being on the point of despair, suddenly within months my whole life had changed again. Was I saved?

Recap on Relationships

What are the main points that we have covered in this chapter? What are the main things you can do to help you have a relationship which brings you balance and calm rather than stress and anxiety?

- When you **invest in your relationship** you get a relationship of pure wealth. Be grateful for what you have and that includes your partner.
- **Compliment your partner from your heart** – praise them for that which you are grateful for.
- **See the positive** rather than the negative in your partner.
- By **making time for yourself on your own** means that you are more relaxed and present with your partner when you are together.
- Find time when you can both **spend time together** doing things that both of you love.
- Communicating well means coming from a calm and balanced space without judgement.
- Start to **accept yourself and your partner for who you and they are** – rather than what you both are not.
- **Be patient with your partner** and see that patience can only be learned when things are not quite going to plan!
- Seeing that **your partner is a reflection of you** – both the good and the bad – so be compassionate to both parties.
- **What to do when things are not going so well**: keep your heart open/ keep lines of communication open/ learn to see what you are giving out you are getting back in return/ be patient – things will change/ give yourselves space to have your own time.
- **Learn to stop arguments by dealing with your emotions before speaking to someone else.** If you speak to someone in anger you are likely to get anger back. Speak from a balanced place and you are more likely to get balance back.

Chapter Seven – Questions

1. What 5 ways can you invest in relationships with others e.g. words of kindness, things you can do, gifts from the heart etc.

2. Write down 5 things that you are grateful for in your partner or in your friends.

3. What ways help you to communicate from a balanced and calm space?

4. Write down a time when you can spend some good time with your partner, or friends (get your diary out now – send the email or text).

5. What things can you do when communication is poor with your partner?

CHAPTER 8

Make Your Home A Sanctuary

Your home has a very important role when it comes to well-being

From personal experience I have found that no matter what is going on around me, as long as my home life is balanced then I can cope. As soon as my home life starts to wobble: noisy neighbours, unpleasant flatmates that is when my stress levels rise.

Essentially what we are working towards is finding the home within. To be able to be in any situation, in any location and still have that peaceful home within you. That is what we are working towards. We are looking at working on both levels – externally and internally. This chapter is focusing on the external.

What you will find by focusing on the external home is that the internal home becomes more peaceful, loving and bright. The following tips should help you to see the importance of your home and will give you some tips on what you can do.

74. Keep Your Home Tidy

Keeping your home tidy comes easy to some and not so easy to others. You will know from experience and looking around you at your living space how you get on in this area. Having a tidy home can make a big difference to how clear you feel and how happy you are. This is not always the case as many compulsive tidiers stress themselves out in the process of tidying. But as a general rule of thumb having a tidy home increases well-being. In the Chinese art of feng shui they say that energy flows better in an ordered and tidy house therefore making happier, more prosperous and healthier inhabitants.

As has been quoted before, Ajahn Chah, the meditation teacher, used to say that you could tell how good a monk's meditation practise was by looking at how clean his kuti (meditation hut) was. He said that it wasn't how many hours you do on the meditation cushion that shows how good your meditation is but how tidy your room is.

Ajahn Chah used to also say that you could tell how good a monastery was at meditating, practising spirituality, and how mindful and internally peaceful they were by looking at how clean their toilets were!

If they couldn't clean up after themselves and take care of the everyday things then he felt that was a sign that they couldn't attend to the own inner peace.

"The outer world is a reflection of the inner world."

"As Above, So Below; As Within, So Without."

I remember when I used to go through rough times in the monastery that one of the senior monks would come into my room. He would look around, see how clean or messy my room was and then say, "You must be okay, Piers, because your room is still tidy".

So having a clean house is really important for your inner life as well. As the monks pointed out to me, your outer world is a reflection of your inner world. Keep your outer world tidy and you help to make your inner world tidy. And vice versa. If you meditate and take care of yourself internally, for example, through following the processes in this book, you help to keep your external world in balance and are therefore more able to cope with things as they arise. By taking care internally you also feel drawn to tidying up or you notice that your house is a mess whereas when you have been lost in your mental stress you have not paid attention to it.

It is therefore important to tidy up after yourself, so both worlds, inner and outer, remain tidy and therefore stress-free.

Obviously don't go to the other extreme and clean at every opportunity which is stressful in itself but do keep things tidy.

A good question to ask yourself is how do you feel when your house is tidy? Good? Well, do it then – do the things that make you feel good.

75. Get Loads of Plants For Your House

Plants, are really good for the bedroom and they are also really good for the rest of the house. Not only do plants look great and are relaxing for the eyes (green, green, green) but they also give off one of the most important thing we humans need. Yes, air!

So fill your house with lovely plants. But please remember to water them. Plants heal. Look how you feel when you are in the countryside. So bring the countryside into your home!

NASA did some experiments several years ago to find out the best way of cleaning air and removing toxins from enclosed spaces, like space stations. And their results? Yes, plants. Below are some of the plants the scientists came up with as most beneficial:

- Bamboo Palm - Chamaedorea Seifritzii
- Chinese Evergreen - Aglaonema Modestum
- English Ivy - Hedera Helix
- Gerbera Daisy - Gerbera Jamesonii
- Janet Craig - Dracaena "Janet Craig"
- Marginata - Dracaena Marginata
- Mass cane/Corn Plant - Dracaena Massangeana
- Mother-in-Law's Tongue - Sansevieria Laurentii
- Pot Mum - Chrysantheium morifolium
- Peace Lily - Spathiphyllum
- Warneckii - Dracaena "Warneckii"

The easiest plant to find and look after is probably the English Ivy although most garden centres will stock a range of these plants. While living in the monastery one of my duties at different times was looking after around 100 plants. Some tips I would pass on for indoor plants are:

- Check the soil for moisture every few days. You do this by touching the soil with your fingertips.
- When the soil around a plant is dry water it
- If it is damp then don't water it as this can rot the roots.

76. Make Your House a Special Space To Live

How much time do you spend in your house? I would say that probably half your life is in your home (8 hours sleeping , 2 hours eating, 2 hours doing other things per day – getting up, getting ready, there at weekends).

What is your house like? Is it tidy, do you care for your house and have you made it a wonderful space to relax, have fun and be stress free?

If not make it so. Remember the adage of the outer reflects the inner… well, make your house a special place to be: keep it clean, buy flowers, get lovely paintings, de-clutter your house, buy plants, repaint it.

And you don't have to spend money making it nice. It doesn't cost anything to clean it or to air it. Even finding 30 minutes or an hour a week will make such a difference to the external space.

Make your home a space where no matter what is going on in the outside world you know you can come back and relax and have a safe haven.

77. Keep Your Home Office in a Separate Room

If you have an office at home then it is important that you have it in a separate room from your sleeping and living arrangements.

Why is this?

Some days it is important to close the office door and not work. Some weeks it is important to have a break, a holiday. If your working space, bills etc. are in front of you all the time then you are more likely to be dragged into that stress.

So keep your home office separate. And if that is not possible then make sure you keep firm boundaries with yourself – don't work all hours God sends. Stop, relax and unwind.

78. Get Crystals For Your Home

Fifteen years ago while working in London I would not have been seen dead with crystals. For a salesman in the City I cared what others thought of me and crystals were not an option! But as I loosened up to life I have realised that I will try anything holistic and if it works then I use it. I am less bothered what people think now. Crystals have worked for me and for thousands if not millions of people across the world they have had a powerful healing affect for them too.

I personally was introduced to the idea of crystals after I had left the monastery. Since then I have learned a lot about the healing properties of crystals. I remember one of the first times I really noticed the benefits of crystals was while I was working in the corporate environment.

I was taking a lunch break and was wandering around the lanes of Brighton where I was working at the time. I wandered into a crystal shop which sold all types of crystals.

I was drawn to a specific crystal which looked really beautiful and picked it up. It was amethyst. I found myself feeling really calm and grounded which was not how I felt walking into the shop. I felt great, time stopped almost. So I bought the crystal and went back to work feeling on top of the world.

And since that day I have always had lots of crystals in my house or in my pockets. Crystals I would recommend are:

- Amethyst (great for balancing and for bedrooms – good for under your pillow to help you sleep)
- Rose quartz (great for healing emotions and for the heart)
- Onyx (good for giving strength when low in energy)
- Iron pyrite (used near computers to lessen the draining effect of them)
- Shungite – this is crystal which comes from Russia and I have found it to be great for when working on a computer.

It is important to cleanse the crystals on a weekly basis. The method for doing this is to place the crystal in a glass of water and leave overnight. Drain off in the morning and then re-use.

79. De-clutter Your House

Once a year it is so important to de-clutter your house. We accumulate things so quickly. And because some of us live such a busy life we don't realise that we are accumulating things. But one or two new things coming into the home every week makes up to a 100 new items lying around your home in a year! And if there are children and spouses involved well that adds up to hundreds of new items every year!

Add that up over a few years and you can see how clutter can build. Have you ever moved house and wondered where all this stuff has come from?

By de-cluttering your house you help to de-clutter your inner world too. With the same force that you hold onto old items of clothing or belongings that you no longer need or use, so you also hold onto old patterns and behaviours within you.

So by practising letting go and de-cluttering your life of items you don't need any more, you are also practising how to let go of your internal processes that don't work for you either. Letting go of external items gives you the confidence to let go of internal patterns. Sometimes we don't know how to let go of internal issues but giving or throwing something away is pretty straight forward (if hard to do for some!). The following exercise will help with this.

EXERCISE 43

De-clutter Your House

1 Go round your house once a year and spring clean. Take a weekend to do this.

2. Find items that you haven't worn, used, listened to, read, watched, or touched for 2 years. It has been shown that if you haven't touched something for 2 years then you are unlikely to touch that item again, except in nostalgia.

3. Make bags to go to the charity shops, and give or throw these items away. By throwing old things away you make space for new better things to enter. By holding onto old items it means that you never have space for better things. And this is also true with the emotions. When you let go of things like anger, or hatred you find that new more healthy emotions like joy and love can then enter your life.

Another benefit of giving things away is that giving from the heart is one of the most joyful feelings ever!

Was I saved? Working in Africa was amazing but I was still not dealing with my issues – my internal hatred, my drinking and my rage. Indeed, on the first night I arrived in Ghana I did what I would precede to do most nights in Ghana – I went drinking. I had been up since 5am and flown from London into the heart of West Africa, but that first night found me partying, drinking and dancing till the early hours of the morning. It was part of the job really. And for the first few months I had an amazing time. I was living in a hostel with the volunteers that I was looking after. There was a group who were a similar age to me who I spent a lot of time with – going out and drinking with.

But when this group had done their 3 months, one by one, they started to leave. A new group arrived, but somehow it was not the same. I made friends with some of them but I started to feel quite lonely. It took quite a lot of effort to connect with new people every few weeks as volunteers came and went. These feelings which I was not dealing with started to intensify. I was not taking care of myself – at all really. I had not really learned how to take care of myself. Sure, I had learned to meditate and still meditated every day, but I had repressed my emotions since the age of 11 and had cried very little since that time.

I had still not understood that my father was an alcoholic and a workaholic at this point so I did what was natural to me in Ghana. I drank and I worked. Looking back now I was doing a very similar job to what my father was doing on board ship in the Royal Navy – he was a supply officer and spent the evenings in the bar socialising and drinking. Once I arrived in Africa I would spend every evening socialising and drinking. I had always felt guilty about drinking on a "school night" - a weekday night, but now I was out drinking with the people I was being paid to look after, it felt okay to be out every night.

I spoke with many people of an evening from the volunteer organisation. There could be up to 100 volunteers in Ghana at anyone time although during my stay it never went above 60. The volunteers would congregate at an American sports bar in the centre of Accra and when they saw me, they would ask questions about their placements, their host families or the company itself. It felt great to be wanted at the beginning. I could drink, socialise and have fun without feeling guilty. From depressed and down I suddenly felt happy and contented that I had something to get my teeth into.

I noticed that some of the company's employees were quite rude and short with the volunteers. When the volunteers would come into our office, most of the employees would ignore them. In hindsight, after spending 8 months there, I could relate to how they were feeling, but still I believed that the volunteers should be honoured and respected. To everyone who came into the office, I would stop what I was doing, and say hello to them by name. Somehow I remembered everyone's name and this meant a lot to people, some of whom had only just turned 18 and were a very long way away from home. I really enjoyed being of service and loved my work at the beginning. It is a strange dichotomy really, looking back now. I knew how to take care of others but I didn't know how to take care of myself...

And living, working and socialising with the volunteers meant that I felt like I was at work most of the time. At home in the volunteer guest house after spending all day with volunteers, I was then bombarded with questions about why the company hadn't done this, why they hadn't done that. At the beginning it made me feel wanted and special – like I was needed. It felt good. But after a few months of 24 hours a day, 7 days a week, I grew jaded. I wanted a break. I made a rule in the boarding house that I didn't speak about work at home and tried to enforce this when out. But it didn't really work when surrounded by volunteers so I used a different tactic and that was to drink as much as I could...

Some nights I would spend all night drinking and go straight from the bar in the morning, back to work again. I would even go back to the bar again later on that same day after work... For some reason the Ghanaian beer didn't give me a hangover so I could drink and drink. Someone mentioned that the beer had formaldehyde in it to stop it spoiling in the heat. Whether this is true or not I didn't know but what I did know was that formaldehyde is used for pickling body parts so maybe that is what I started to do to my body...

In all it was a pretty intense time. It is interesting recalling my experience now after all these years because many of the experiences seemed to have faded until I started to put these words down. An event which had a huge impact across the world happened while I was in Ghana.

After I had been in Ghana for about a month I got invited by one of the other volunteer managers to a football match between the 2 biggest rival football teams – Accra Hearts of Oak and Asante Kotoko. I agreed to go but then when the day arrived I realised that as the country manager would be away there would be no-one in the office so agreed to stay at work. Many of the volunteers were going as this was renowned for being an amazing match. I agreed to meet up with the volunteers after the match in the American sports bar.

As I sat there in the bar waiting for the volunteers, reports started to come in that someone had died at the match. Then reports said a couple of people had died. I hoped at that point that the volunteers were okay. Then the reports intensified – 10 people had died, then 50, then 100 and then hundreds! I was shocked and didn't really know what to do. I started calling on my mobile but mobile calling at that time was useless – maybe 5% of my calls would get through or get connected. I sat and I waited. At last some of the volunteers showed up and they said that they had left at half time as there were so many people at the match, and they couldn't see anything. They had not seen any trouble. The final death toll was 127 people.

Over the next few days I visited, called and checked that all the volunteers were safe. And amazingly all the volunteers had been down the opposite end from the tragedy. Some had witnessed what had happened but all had been safe. It felt a pretty stressful time, but it felt good to be of service and to be strong for others. To this day, the events of May 9th 2001 is still the biggest football disaster in African history.

Another event which really rocked me happened a few months later. It was a Saturday and I was in Accra. One of the volunteers called me or left a message with a friend. She said she needed to meet up with me and that something bad had happened. We met at a bar and she brought one of her volunteer friends with her. As the conversation unfolded it turned out that this friend, Matilda, had been attacked. One of the bar owners had attacked her. I felt incensed and very protective. I wanted to confront the bar owner and get the police involved. But Matilda wouldn't hear of it. I wasn't allowed to tell anyone about it. For a day I felt a huge weight on my shoulders. I couldn't say anything, talk with anyone about it or do anything. It felt really intense. Eventually with consent from the girls I confronted the attacker. I remember standing on the side of the road by his bar on Labadi Ring Road, one of the main roads into Accra with cars zooming past. I kept my cool but let him know that his behaviour was not acceptable. I was livid inside and wanted to hit him but I had learned about suppressing emotions and contained myself. I banned people from his bar but couldn't say why – I think I made up an excuse about him not being a good man.

After a few days, the girls gave me the go ahead to speak to my manager. Someone else needed to know. It felt a huge relief to unburden myself from this load. The manager took on the full responsibility and dealt with the attacker himself.

Although these events made me feel needed it also gave me the feeling that I just couldn't stop. No matter where I was in the country, be it Accra, Kumasi or Tamale I would bump into volunteers and I would go into manager role. I needed a break. I started to have more and more time away from the volunteers and so most weekends I would go to the local beach resort of Krokrobite where I would swim and unwind.

But being white in an African country added to my sense of never being able to switch off. Being white in an African country felt to me what it must be like to be famous. Everywhere I went I stood out. People shouted "abruni" at me when I walked down the street which is the Ghanaian term for "white man". They would point and stare. Kids would run after me. When I walked in town, people would come up to me and ask for money. I started to feel that I couldn't get away. I needed to get away, but how?

Many of the ex-pats (Westerners) who were working there said to me that it didn't cause them any problems. I wondered if it was just me but listening one day to an English marketing director who was working for Nestle I realised that they were all living sheltered lives. This Englishman was complaining that he had gone shopping at a different supermarket and had been hassled by loads of people in the car park trying to sell him things. It sounded like everyday life for me and most of the volunteers – we weren't driven around in air-conditioned 4x4s from our air-conditioned homes to our air-conditioned offices. We travelled by local transport with the locals and ate in the local restaurants. But the consequence of doing it "local" style meant that we stood out like a sore thumb.

One thing I did notice during the time I lived in Africa was the fact that when I felt good then nobody would hassle me. Looking back now I see that this was another example of law of attraction. When I felt good, I was smiling, happy inside and then I attracted to me smiles and happy people being drawn to me. When, on the other hand, I felt terrible, miserable, depressed, wanting to be alone, and be left alone – this was when I was hassled all the time. Stood at a bus stop I would be asked for money, walking down the street I would be shouted at or hassled to buy things. Africa was initiating me into the laws of the universe. Looking back now

I see the importance of doing all that I can do to make myself feel good. If I am leaving for work and I don't feel good then it is my responsibility to lift myself into a better feeling space. If I don't do this then I will attract to me those situations that match how I am feeling. As Africa was showing me – law of attraction works – by feeling good I was attracting great things and by feeling bad, likewise, I was attracting challenging situations.

The more time I spent in Africa the more I started to struggle mentally. I was struggling to switch off. Being with the volunteers day in and day out, 7 days a week started to take its toll. I began to feel that I was going crazy. I wanted to get away, I wanted to stop but I didn't know who to communicate this to or if I should communicate this with anyone. I had learned at boarding school to not speak of my weaknesses, so rather than communicate with anyone I carried on. Eventually it became too much and I asked to move out of the volunteer hostel and move somewhere smaller and closer to the centre of town. The hostel had been based on the outskirts of Accra in Teshi-Nungha which meant a long, sweaty commute stuck in gridlocked traffic for at least an hour. Moving to the district of Osu, in the centre of town meant that I could walk home. I was still living with one other volunteer, but this change meant that I was able to relax a little bit.

At the weekends going to the beach resort at Krokrobite helped to de-stress me. An English lady had set up a type of youth hostel/ village with huts and restaurant right next to the beach. It was a beautiful spot with a surf break so each weekend I would travel a couple of hours along the coast and spend the weekend swimming, surfing and eating well. I went tee-total at the weekend and it was lovely to start to become clearer in my thoughts. The changes made a difference and I moved away from the edge of insanity, but still I felt like a mess inside. I didn't know what else to do. Here I was living in paradise, but it anything but that for me.

After I had been in Ghana for 4 months, the managing director of the company came out to trouble shoot a project in one of the local countries. The manager in Togo was having conflict with many of the volunteers and as I spoke French, was asked by the MD to go and spend a week helping the manager get the Summer school project off the ground. The volunteers were mainly working in schools, which in Summer time, were on a break. The volunteers were paying to teach and there was no students to teach so they came up with the idea of starting up a free school for the local kids. The problem was that the country manager, who was

Togolese, had done nothing to organise the summer school. We had a week or so before the end of term. Time was short.

I arrived in Togo, which is situated on the border of Ghana, and was met by the country manager. Togo was originally a French colony and it felt on arrival, in the capital Lomé, very different to the old British colony of Ghana. There were cafés, croissants, and coffee. And I was transported around the town in a very French way – on the back on a moped taxi! I was taken to my hotel and left to settle. I felt quite lonely, here in my hotel, in another country. I ate alone in the restaurant which was nestled outside in the hotel's gardens. It was not recommended that a Westerner wander around at night-time; political unrest meant that it was not a safe thing to do.

The local manager was a real challenge to work with. I came from a Western perspective and he came from an African perspective. I was very driven to get results; he was relaxed and if the summer school worked, so be it, and if not so be it. I found it incredibly frustrating. After the first few days of the manager being on best behaviour for me, he slipped into his normal routine. "I'll meet you at 9am at the hotel..." I don't remember what time he would eventually turn up but it was more like 11am. I sat and I waited. My frustration levels grew. He was clearly lying to me and to the volunteers. I was tempted to tell the MD to fire him.

Looking back now I see that he was a great teacher. I see that all situations in our lives are great teachers. Ajahn Brahm, a disciple of Ajahn Chah, talks about how everything is a teacher (Ajahn) and you can call them so, e.g. Ajahn "Wife", Ajahn "Tummy Ache". So here in Togo I was being presented with an Ajahn – Ajahn Togo Manager. He was teaching me how stressed I was, he was teaching me that I was so focused on the destination that I didn't care about the path. I didn't care that I was miserable as hell – I wanted to get the Summer school open. He was teaching me patience.

Unfortunately I didn't see any of this at the time. So eventually I had a big argument with him about how he was managing the country. I see that he was very frightened. Here I had been sent by the MD to keep an eye on him and he was frightened that I would fire him. But somehow my presence bucked him into making the effort that was needed to get the Summer school going. After a week I left to return to Ghana – job done really.

On return I spoke to the MD about the situation and we both agreed that it would be foolhardy to fire the country manager although, I believe he said that he would keep an eye on the situation. For a time I thought I might be sent to Togo to run the project there which filled me with both excitement and fear. I really needed a break. My mind was a mess. I needed to stop and the life I was currently living – being with volunteers all the time was exasperating the situation intensely. The MD was really impressed by my work and had had many amazing reports from the returning volunteers about how helpful I was to them. He therefore didn't want me to leave. He offered me a bonus to go on holiday and allowed me to take 2 weeks leave. I was immensely relieved. Finally, I could stop. I could stop without having volunteers hassling me all the time.

I spent the first week of my holiday sat on a beach in the beautiful resort of Busia, on the Western border of Ghana. It was wonderful just to stop, to swim, sleep and eat. I still felt emotionally fragile, but the break without volunteers helped to take me away from the edge. I was seeing that I found it hard to say no. I was always available for people at the cost of my own health. I was of service to others, but not to myself. I felt I didn't deserve kindness.

The second week of my holiday I travelled inland and visited different cities. I also visited the national park which had elephants, baboons and other amazing wildlife. It wasn't Kenya, but I could say I had visited a game reserve. My overriding feeling was of loneliness. I felt lonely in Africa. I couldn't communicate with people, nor do I think they would have been able to hear me; I needed the company of people and yet I couldn't handle being with them either.

I returned to Accra, feeling rested, although aware that I was still struggling. I started to go swimming most days to keep fit and found a meditation centre run by a group called the Brahma Kumaris. I was pretty sceptical of the group being where I was at and after being told to meditate on my 3rd eye, in the centre of my forehead, I found this exasperated my feeling of being crazy. I started to become paranoid. Later on I would realize that meditating on the 3rd eye is not recommended for a mentally unstable person (the energy needs to leave the head and more come into the body).

Although my drinking habits had eased I still went out on binges from time to time. One weekday night I was out in my local bar with a Western friend. I ended up with a woman from Sierra Leon. I had been questioning my sexuality since I had split up from my ex-girlfriend the year before. Indeed, this had been a big reason for the split – I needed to know whether I was gay or not. This liaison with this African lady made me realize that I loved being with women. It was an amazing experience.

Later on that week I was in the same bar hungry for more sexual experiences. I was dancing with a woman who I found attractive. She turned out to be a prostitute. I didn't have enough money on me for her rates so borrowed some money from my friend. I went back to her hotel which was quite dingy. She went into her room, woke her room mate/ boyfriend up who was sleeping in the bed and he left. It felt incredibly weird, but I was being stubborn so followed through with it. I could see she wasn't interested in me and she kept looking at her watch as we had sex. It was a devastating experience and in the following days as I realised that I had contracted a sexual disease from her, I felt as bad as I had felt in Africa. I hated myself. How could I be so stupid? I now had this infection on my face. The doctors didn't have a clue what it was and gave me iodine to put on it. It took months to clear up so I carried this purple face around for ages – it felt humiliating. It was only when I got home months later did one of my friends, who was a medical student, say that I had herpes – a cold sore. Once I started with the correct medication my cold sore cleared up within a week.

Whether this was the final straw I am not sure but it was around this time that I decided that I had had enough of Africa. I spoke with Head Office in the UK and tended my resignation. I had been in Africa 8 months – it could well have been 8 years by all I had fitted into my time. And yet, yes it was time to go. On the day I left I woke in the night feeling nauseous. I started to vomit. And couldn't stop vomiting for hours. My body had seized up and I could hardly walk. It took me 30 minutes to walk a 5 minute journey to the local doctor. I sat in the waiting room for hours groaning. When the doctor saw me he put me on a drip and I stayed that way sleeping for a few hours.

I woke in the afternoon feeling much better. The nausea had gone. I rushed back home, packed my bag, bought a few presents, dropped in to say goodbye to colleagues before heading out to the airport. One of my Ghanaian colleagues came to the airport with me. He earned roughly £25 a month, which was a good salary out there. I gave him a gift of £50 which came to me spur of the moment – he was very tearful and appreciative.

At what point the nausea returned, I don't remember but on the flight home I filled several sick bags. I didn't know what was wrong with me – maybe I had malaria, maybe alcohol poisoning. I arrived in the UK and asked my mother to take me straight to the doctor. My African journey had finished but I still had a way to go before I would be healed...

Recap on Reducing Stress in Your Home

Your home is a really important aspect of your life. A peaceful home life signifies greatly reduced levels of stress.

What points have we covered in this chapter?

- **It is really important to keep your home tidy**. Keeping your house tidy helps to keep your emotions and your mind ordered and calm – you're not always worrying about the mess in the house.

- **Plants have been proven to add oxygen** and to take out unnecessary chemicals from the spaces they are in. Plants are therefore a great way of making your home a more relaxed and calm space.

- Most of us use our homes like a railway station – a stopping place between work, and going out. By **taking the time to buy flowers, paint the walls and to dust** means that your home becomes a place you enjoy unwinding in rather than stressing in.

- If you have an office at home try to keep the space in a separate room. This helps you to switch off when you are not working.

- Crystals have been used for thousands of years to help balance environments. **Use crystals to in your own dwelling to bring peace** and calm to your own home environment.

- **By de-cluttering your home** you give yourself not only a tidier home, but you also give yourself the space for new, better things to enter.

Chapter Eight – Questions

1. Write a list of things that you haven't used for 2 years or more & are not likely to use again for 2 years. Visualize yourself giving them away to someone who will use them and love them. How do you feel? Now give them away.

2. Name 3 plants that will help you to improve the atmosphere and air in your home and office.

3. Name 5 ways you could improve your house to make it more homely e.g. flowers, plants etc.

CHAPTER 9
Deepening Your Rest & Sleep

Rest and sleep are vital for keeping on top of stress. It is a time that your body must have in order to heal from the day's activities.

And when you don't get a good night's sleep for several days you feel it on all levels: physically – you feel tired, mentally – you find it hard to think clearly, and emotionally – you are quick to anger and more prone to tears and upset.

So creating the right environment to sleep well is paramount to keeping your stress levels down. The following will help you to sleep well again.

80. The Importance of Getting a Good Night's Sleep

As a society and as individuals we go through phases of focusing on certain areas of our lives – from exercise to hobbies, from diets to work. But as a society we spend very little time on sleep unless of course we can't sleep. We have probably all been through phases where we couldn't sleep but generally it is rare that we give focus on being a better sleeper or getting deeper, more profound sleep. Interesting... And yet considering we spend a third of every day sleeping it seems strange that there aren't thousands of courses teaching us better sleep – there are certainly thousands of courses teaching us how to be better managers.

The difference between getting a good night's sleep and not is huge – from high productivity to low productivity, from feeling centred and balanced to irritable and snappy. And yet there are so many things you can do to improve your sleep. We will cover quite a few in this chapter. Sleep plays a huge part in your life and therefore it's importance cannot be stated enough.

Indeed, my stay at the monastery was a tumultuous time on many levels. I really struggled to get by day-to-day for about 2 years – I would cry every day, and was incredibly unkind to myself during that period – I self-harmed and punched most inanimate objects from rocks, to wood and yes, made several visits to A&E to repair myself... The anger that I had been suppressing from childhood flew out of me like a hurricane. And there seemed little I could do to stop it.

And yet the interesting thing was that my sleep was not that badly effected. The abbot would ask me on a regular basis, "How are you sleeping, Piers?" Generally I slept really well so told him. There were instances where I would be awake into the night but this was very rare.

The abbot's question, I feel, was in order to see how bad I was. And if I was sleeping well, well then the abbot saw that I was doing okay – even if I wasn't the most pleasant of people to live with...

This is the importance of sleep.

So what is the secret of getting a good night's sleep?

81. How To Get A Good Night's Sleep 1: Meditation.

Meditate before you go to sleep. You will find that if your mind is too chaotic then you will not be able to sleep. Meditation helps to switch the mind off – to unplug so to speak

So it is recommended that you meditate before you go to sleep. Even 5 minutes of meditation can help to turn the mind off. What happens with some people is that they go to bed really wired and buzzing and fall asleep because they are so exhausted. On a scientific level they are in beta brainwave which the brain operates in most of the day. They fall asleep in beta. If anything wakes them in the night then they go straight back into beta – thinking, analysing, worrying.

By unplugging the mind with meditation you allow the mind to drop into alpha brainwaves which has a slower cycles per second. If you wake in the night then it is much easier to drop back to sleep again as the mind is already unplugged. I believe most people wake in the night but those with settled and still minds go back to sleep again within seconds. Those with busy minds wake up because their minds start to race.

Meditating before sleep can be the difference between sleeping well and having fitful sleep. The difference to the rest of your life can be amazing. We know the effects of sleeping really poorly, as mentioned above, but the effects of sleeping well are wonderful to behold as well – feeling vibrant, energized, clear thinking, balanced emotions, a positive outlook on life.

And it might only take 5 minutes...

When I left the monastery I found that I had trouble sleeping. There were so many stimuli which meant that I couldn't switch off at the end of the day. I had been living in unpopulated areas for 4 years and had spent 6 months of my time in the monastery in silence. Suddenly I was living in a big city with lots of people, lots of noises, movement and distraction. And I was finding it really hard to sleep. I just wasn't used to sleeping in a place where there was noise at night.

One of my tricks to switch off and sleep was to meditate. Okay, so I meditated for 2 hours but my brain was just not used to having any form of stimulation and needed that time to "let go"...

Give it a go – try it for a month and see how you feel in yourself and in your life. Get into a regular daily routine with it and you will see your sleep levels affecting the rest of your life in a really positive way.

82. How To Get A Good Night's Sleep 2: One Hour Twilight Zone

What is the one hour twilight zone? Good question!

The one hour twilight zone is making the hour before you go to bed a time for little activity. This means that you turn off the TV, stop listening to music unless it is relaxing or meditation music. Turn computers off and breathe deeply.

This also means that you don't read any really exciting books. Reading a spiritual or self-help book really helps to calm the mind down. You will probably find that you want to go to sleep before the hour is up – that's great!

I always find I feel so peaceful reading self-help books. Why is that? Because you are feeling the energy of the writer; if they are kind, loving beings then that is the energy you pick up. Read a horror and you pick up and feel horror!

Also in the One Hour Twilight Zone try to stay clear of really heavy discussions with people, this again stimulates the brain. So turn your phone off and relax. You've done well for the day so let yourself unwind.
What you are starting to accomplish in this hour is a slowing down. As we have just mentioned about brainwaves, in this hour you start to move gently into alpha brainwave. This means that sleep, which takes you into theta and delta brainwaves, is just a step away, rather than a jump. You are slowly lowering yourself into the peaceful waters of your unconscious.

The twilight hour is a gentle, quiet period, a transitional time. In the West, we jump hecticly from one activity to the next. And in the same way we do that with sleep in that we tire ourselves out so that we can hardly keep our eyes open any more out of sheer exhaustion. The twilight hour allows a peaceful and natural unfolding – you are preparing yourself for the most important part of the day, a part of the day where you heal, release stresses, regather your strength, allow the body to do what it does best and rest, and allow the mind to reorder and release thoughts.

83 How To Get A Good Night's Sleep 3: Sacred Sleeping Space

Make the place where you sleep a place where this is all you do. Take out televisions and electrical equipment, especially computers. Your sleeping space should be a sacred space where you rest, meditate and be intimate with your loved one but these things only.

Your sleeping space should not be where you work. You will be more prone to waking in the night, worrying about work if you do.

Get some plants into your room. They are a wonderful way of changing the energy and air in your room. A list of wonderful plants (which we have spoken about before) are as follows:

- English ivy – helix hedera
- Spider plants
- Dracaena
- Boston ferns
- Fig trees (ficus benjanmina)

By having the colour green in your room, bringing the outdoors in, can be very relaxing and it adds to the sacredness of your room. A room which is peaceful, beautifully adorned with wonderful hangings, crystals and candles can be so soothing to sleep in. Do you feel relaxed just thinking about such a calming room?

Having a room which is overflowing with clothes and clutter and is not clean does not induce the same feeling of calm. Our rooms can be like this because we don't notice any more – we are just too busy. So take the time, tidy your room, throw things out, make your bedroom into a sacred space and watch your sleep blossom.

84. What To Do If You Can't Sleep?

If you find that you are tossing and turning and can't sleep then get up or sit upright in bed. Meditate until your mind settles and you feel tired.

If this doesn't work read something really uplifting or spiritual. Don't read books which are stimulating, like racy novels or thrillers, and leave the TV alone. Both of these are very stimulating and will only prolong your insomnia.

One trick I use, especially if there is external noise around is to do the following. **I tell myself that I am just relaxing and don't need to sleep**. This seems to take away the need and worry about sleeping and I fall asleep straight away.

Another trick is to do deep breathing and try to make yourself stay awake. I haven't tried this but have heard insomniacs who swear by this! They find that by trying to stay awake they fall asleep straight away.

85. Have A Lie-in A Couple Of Times A Week

If you are working a 9-5 job or looking after your kids your routine is going to be getting up early most of the week. In order to reduce your stress levels it is really important for the body to catch up on sleep at least once a week. If you have children then take it in turns with your partner to look after the kids while the other person sleeps at the weekend. One of you could lie in Saturday, while the other sleeps in on Sunday.

Failing that, get into a routine whereby the kids know that you are not to be disturbed on the weekend mornings. Kids learn really quickly. If they know that if they wake early they can just play quietly in their room for a while that will help to give you a little extra sleep.

If you find it really hard to get a lie-in then try to go to bed early. If you have kids, then go to bed soon after they have gone to sleep. This will enable you to catch up on sleep. What we can do when looking after children is feel that, "now they are asleep, I can actually get things done," and you go into busy mode. Some evenings this is fine but every evening will lead to falling asleep in exhaustion.

Another thing when children fall asleep is the feeling it's my time and we then use it rather ineffectively by being on Facebook or surfing the internet. Use the period after children go to sleep to do a twilight hour. Really take care of yourself.

And by having a lie-in helps you to wake naturally, when the body, mind and spirit is ready to wake. On a scientific level the brain needs a certain amount of time in delta and theta brainwaves in order to stay mentally healthy and sane. Having restless and fitful sleep means that the brain is not getting sufficient access to these brainwaves. But by sleeping in you allow your brain to get as much of the slower, more restorative brainwaves as it needs.

86. Use A Black Out Sheet On Your Windows

Certain sleep therapists swear by having no light in a room while you are sleeping.

This is something that I usually do and find that I am able to sleep so much better if

I am not woken up by light streaming into my room or through electrical displays.

Certain people like to be woken up by the morning light but if you are not sleeping then blacking the windows out might help you to sleep through the night. Another solution is to get a blackout mask for the face. This is again something that I use when I am travelling and find that this helps me to get a good night's sleep. Find what suits you best and use that.

87. What To Do If There Is Noise At Night?

Noise can be quite disturbing to sleep so it is important to find a remedy for this. There are several different options with noise:

1. Earplugs: Simple solution and doesn't take long to put them in. The easiest solution and one I have used for many years, for many years wonderful sleep!

2. Getting used to the noise: If you have just moved house and are living next to a busy road you might find it difficult to sleep to start off with. But with time you will not notice the noise and will sleep through any disturbances.
   I have personally found that it takes me about 2 weeks to get used to a new situation. If I find challenges in those 2 weeks I just tell myself that I am in this 2 weeks' window and to be patient with myself. I recently lived next to a main road and found that after a few days I didn't even notice there was traffic; I slept really well.

3. Noisy neighbours. This is a challenging one. I have lived next to noisy neighbours and found that what kept me awake was my mind rather than the noise itself.

   I found that it was my mind saying, "Oh they shouldn't be making noise like that etc. etc…"

   But as soon as I settled my mind down and saw that they were probably enjoying themselves and having a good time then I just fell asleep.

   If you do go and ask them to turn the music down or be quieter be quite sure that you are not really angry. Calm yourself down and ask them politely or you could cause more stress.

My rule of thumb has been that if people are having a one-off party then I am okay with that and let them get on with it. If it is all the time then I would consider speaking to them about it.

4. Snoring partners. What do you do if your partner snores? Earplugs is an option but it is important to speak with your partner. Let them know that you can't sleep and that you will nudge them in the night if they do start snoring.

   Find out what positions they snore in (usually on their backs) and ask them to try sleeping in other positions the next day when you speak to them. Once they get used to sleeping in a different position (probably a couple of days) this should remedy the situation.

   Getting an ergonomic pillow (one which is designed for the neck and back) is another way that people have remedied snoring problems. Having the neck supported means that the breathing channels are clear and the snoring stops.

   Another option is to get up and sleep in another room if your partner is keeping you awake. Remember how important sleep is to your stress levels and don't spend hours getting frustrated and stressed when all is takes is one minute to get up and go and sleep in the next room.

   But saying that remember the power of the mind. If you want the snoring to wake you then it will. What do I mean by that? Well when you think about and focus on how annoying the snoring is then when you hear it you will feel annoyed – as if it is something against you. When on the other hand you think about all the wonderful qualities of your partner rather than just focusing on the snoring then you will find that it won't wake you any more. And if it does start focusing on their wonderful qualities.

   Try it. What have you got to lose if your partner does snore?

88. Beds and Bedding

What is your bed and your bedding like? Is it warm and comfortable or hard, uncomfortable and lumpy? Having a comfortable but also well supported bed is very important for getting a good night's sleep. If you are not comfortable or too cold then this will affect your sleep patterns. Invest in your sleep and you will reap the rewards in the rest of your life.

Tip: Making your bed more comfortable

A simple and cheap solution to making a mattress more comfortable is to put a duvet or blanket underneath the sheet and onto the mattress. Being comfortable does make a difference to sleep and this is something that you can do now.

89. Having Your Bedroom The Right Temperature

Having your bedroom too hot or too cold will make a difference to how well you sleep. You will keep waking up if the room sways into either extreme.

The ideal temperature is 60-65° Fahrenheit (16-18° c). One way of maintaining this is to have a little heater in the room in winter and put it on a low setting. Try things out, and see what works for you. Adapt it to your own needs.

If you have a partner who likes the room hotter or colder than you then try and find a compromise. Rather than one of you sleeping well at the expense of the other try to find a middle ground. For the one who gets too cold try wearing more clothing and try wearing socks or have a hot water bottle or an electric blanket which heats your side only.

90. Drinking Camomile Tea and Keeping Off Caffeine and Chocolate

Drinking caffeinated drinks like coca cola, coffee, tea or hot chocolate are likely to keep you awake at night. Try not to drink caffeinated drinks after 5pm in the afternoon if you have trouble sleeping or if you want to see how it changes the way you sleep.

In my own experience I have found that if I drink coffee or tea late at night then I won't sleep very well. I remember on several occasions going to a party and drinking coca cola all night only to find that I couldn't then sleep later on.

What I do recommend to drink before going to sleep is camomile tea. Camomile tea calms the mind and body and ready's it for sleep. You can buy camomile tea with honey or vanilla which tastes lovely as well.
Remember though that if you drink lots before going to bed then you are more likely to wake in the night in order to go to the toilet. Again find the balance for your life.

91. Digesting Your Meal For Several Hours Before Sleep

I have heard the expression that the body uses the same amount of energy to digest a heavy meal as it does to walk up a mountain!
So it is very important to have plenty of time between having a heavy meal and going to bed. If there is not this period you will find that you are kept awake by the extensive workings of your stomach!

Ideally it would be best to have a light meal in the evening around 6pm if you are intending on going to sleep between 10pm and 11pm. Become aware of your patterns and see how you feel the day after a heavy meal.

92. Breathing Deeply If You Do Wake In The Night

If you wake in the middle of the night then start to get into the habit of breathing deeply. Not only will this calm you down but it will also send you straight back off to sleep again.

If you wake in the night, imagine that you are so relaxed and calm, and then feel yourself sinking deeper into your bed. Breathe deeply and relax.

EXERCISE 44

Belly Breathing For Sleep

If you wake in the night try this belly breathing technique. Try it now so that you are familiar with it if you do wake. You don't need to move or sit upright unless you have been awake for some time.

1. Move both hands onto your belly. Place your hands 2 fingers breadth below your bellybutton. Make a conscious effort to breathe into the stomach. See if you can make the stomach rise and fall.

2. Imagine the rise and fall is like being in a boat and feeling the rise and fall of the ocean: gentle, relaxing and powerful. Feel yourself floating, drifting and allow your mind to relax and follow this gentle rhythmical movement.

3. Keep breathing deeply as you become aware of your breath. Allow your breath to soften and deepen and become one with the ocean. Let all tension be dissolved into the water. Relax and let your breath slow even further, relaxing you even deeper. You are an amazing being. Allow yourself to drift off to sleep.

I flew in from Ghana and was met at the airport by my mother. On the journey back to my mother's house from the airport, my mother informed me that my grandmother and great aunt had died in the last week. My grandfather had lost his sister and wife within a few days. I went immediately into my rescuer mode and although I was feeling physically pretty terrible having spent most of my flight being physically sick, I offered to spend some time with him. It was now the end of 2001.

He lived on Dartmoor, which is remote moorland region in the South West of the UK. As I sat in my room late at night in the silence of Winter I realized how much of a mess I was. For the past few years I had been trying to help others, but here, now, I knew that I needed to start helping myself. I couldn't be of help to anyone now. I felt I was going crazy – I could literally hear the voices running round my head at a million miles an hour while sat in this dark silence. I knew I needed help. I knew I needed a break, I just didn't know where or how.

I had one last throw of the dice and spent New Year in Edinburgh and the north of England with friends from Ghana. I drank and drank. In a period of 2 weeks I spent about £1000 on drink and clubs.

Finally I'd had enough. I had not seen the sunlight for a week having been going to bed at sunrise and being woken up after dark. I was staying in a pub and was drinking on waking till going to bed. I got in touch with a family friend who was living locally to the pub I was in. I went to stay for a week and it was a life saver – clean sheets, sunlight, good food, and abstaining from alcohol was like waking up from a nightmare to see that everything is all right. My friend let me use the internet and phone to research some places to stay. I phoned a local monastery to her (an hour's drive) but they were on Winter retreat and weren't taking guests. My friend talked about driving up and visiting but other things came up.

I sent off for information for several retreat centres and then set off south feeling 100% better. But I got distracted as I usually did. I was addicted to football and agreed to meet some friends in Leeds on the way down so I could watch my team Portsmouth play against Bradford City.

The game was awful and having started to drink early and being of very loud voice I started to verbally abuse the referee. I was like some animal. I was aware of watching myself getting carried into this destructive behaviour. It felt horrible being there. I didn't fit in and never had, but there stood on the terraces I realized that I was starting to cross a line, one I didn't want to cross. It was the last football match I ever attended.

My friends and I caught the train back to London after the match and we went for a drink in King's Cross. The pub turned out to be a strippers pub and as I stood there in the crowd of men I realized how frightened and unhappy these girls were. My heart opened just a fraction and I started to send them healing and wish them well. What on earth was I doing with my life? I needed out of this quickly but was struggling to let go.

I returned to my mother's house in Portsmouth and found that the information I had requested for the retreat centres had come through. I booked a 3 week retreat in Devon and set off.

The retreat centre was eye opening and life changing. The glimpse I had of being a mess consolidated itself. I was a complete mess. I was a time bomb waiting to go off. I had used every tool in the book to suppress my feelings. I had a huge insight into the fact that I had only ever loved my first dog – I didn't love anyone else. My heart was shut tight like a clam. I also realized how deeply I hated my boarding school. I found 2 books which referenced the boarding school I had attended and both were disparaging. I delved deeper into my feelings about my boarding school experience over the next few weeks and started to uncover a river of rage and hatred. I started to lose the plot – the voices intensified in my head and I started seeing visions in my meditations of death. I had to find a place to heal and quickly.

Again, I knew what I wanted, like with Africa. I knew that I wanted a place I could go for an indefinite time and receive board and lodgings in return for work.

The gears of law of attraction kicked into action and synchronicity after synchronicity unfolded until I was led to speaking to the Abbot of a Buddhist monastery in the north of England. I agreed to go and cook for 10 days. Northumberland for me was near Norwich which was a short journey away, but the synchronicities lined up again when I realized that the monastery I had contacted a few weeks earlier and had spoken about visiting was the same place

I was going to cook now! I was returning north but no longer with the idea of going on a drinking binge.

I popped into my mother's house for a few days on the journey north so that I could pick a few belongings up. There I received a message that I had been offered the manager's job for the volunteer organisation in Thailand. I understood that I would have an amazing salary (a Western salary in a cheap place like Thailand would be great riches), a house, a car and full responsibility for the whole country. What a career opportunity! But I wasn't so sure – my friends and family all said how I was obviously going to take the Thai job, but they couldn't see the state of my emotions and mind... I had agreed to help at the monastery for 10 days and I would honour that. After the 10 days were up I would make a decision. My life was about to change again.

Arriving at the monastery was like arriving home. Not to a parent's home but to a spiritual home. Suddenly I was surrounded by good people, really good people. And good people who cared. I arrived with 2 bags and intended to stay the 10 days.

As the 10 days unfolded I realised that I wasn't going anywhere. I might have the opportunity of a lifetime to be the country manager for an international organisation, but here I was being offered the opportunity of many lifetimes! The chance to stay in a Buddhist monastery. The irony of being offered to be the Thai manager or live in a Thai monastery was not lost on me. It felt like I was being tested to see whether I would bite on the big red juicy cherry or finally face what I had spent a long time running from. I committed to staying in the monastery and agreed to become the office manager for a year. I felt very honoured and it felt 100% the right thing to do. I started to have huge insights and spiritual awakenings into the nature of reality and the impermanence of it all. At one point I became aware that everything was made up of energy and could literally see it before my eyes. After each insight I would go running to the Abbot to tell him the latest awakening I had had. But he would act as if he hadn't heard or as if it were no big deal. The deeper I understood the teachings the greater I realised that the more I got attached to the amazing experiences the more I would get attached to the bad experiences if they were to arrive. Unfortunately for me I got attached to the amazing experiences so when the bad experiences arrived, boy did I know it!

After a period of 4 months I decided that seeing as I had already committed to the office manager's job I might as well ask to become a Novice (Postulant) monk. I was accepted.

Whether having the safe container of the monastic vows or the safety of the monastery itself, something shifted and something shifted big style. I had stopped. Yes, I had finally stopped running. My ego started to go crazy. On my 26th birthday no big fuss was made. "I" baked my own cake, "I" had to work, "I" couldn't do what I wanted, "I" couldn't go out.

The self harming started.

Just a trickle to start off with. I started to punch thistle and nettles. I was enraged. Little things would trigger me and I just couldn't stop myself. My mind became like an enraged tiger – I would fill up with this passionate hatred and anger and rage. The rage I had suppressed growing up with an aggressive alcoholic father, the rage I had suppressed at boarding school started to spew forth violently. The part which had protected me so well for so many years started to feel extremely threatened. Instead of protecting me, it now started to bully me, trying to force me back into the same relationship we had had. But I couldn't do it any more. I didn't want to do it any more. I didn't want to hold this rage in so that it carried on poisoning me.

The consequence was that I started to punch walls, blocks of wood, rocks and telegraph poles. I started to beat the hell out of myself, bashing my head and body with my fists.

All that I had been using to suppress this inner hatred and rage was no longer available: no sex, no alcohol, no TV, no internet, no football, no pornography, no newspaper (apart from Sunday's), no music... It was like going cold turkey from years of abuse. Cold turkey from drugs can last between 5 to 10 days. For me my cold turkey lasted a few years.

Every few months I would use excessive force on myself during this time, try and commit suicide or run away from the monastery. Sometimes I would end up in casualty in the local hospital; broken fist, knife wounds, broken feet (this was an accident falling down the stairs) and those injuries I never told anyone about: cracked ribs, another broken or fractured fist and cuts all across my body.

I tried suicide time and time again but the razor-blades or knives would only sink so deep before I would start sobbing uncontrollably so that I could no longer hold the cutting implement. As I learned more about Buddhism I realised that to commit suicide would be, according to their beliefs, the worst thing possible. I would literally be transported to a hell realm by committing suicide. I couldn't do that either.

Now why would the monastery put up with me? Why would they not throw me out? I was pretty disruptive to say the least. I asked this question recently while on a return visit to the monastery. One of the senior monks said how hard I worked and how much I did give to the monastery. Indeed although in my own time I was abusing myself, in the work period I worked ceaselessly – cooking, gardening, writing, doing the accounts, and paperwork. And never did my rage get primarily directed at anyone. Indirectly yes I must have been horrible to be around but never did I shout, raise my voice or hurt anyone else.

At one point one of the junior monks was very aggressive with me but instead of directing anything at him, I walked up the stairs, punched a hole in the wall, walked to my room and then proceeded to punch myself around the head till I nearly knocked myself out. I then put on my coat, politely said goodbye to this monk and went outside and walked all day. Community living can be challenging. Without wisdom we can project our baggage onto others and blame them for it. With wisdom we can see the community as a way of working through our "stuff." It took me many years and several fall outs before I started to see the teaching in community.

Another reason I felt that they let me stay was because some of the senior monks had had tough times when they were junior monks themselves. They knew just what I was going through and their hearts opened in compassion. The monks were amazing. I repeat the monks were absolutely amazing. I have never known such unconditional giving as they gave to me me (I have to say my wife is pretty much on a par with them now).

I should have been locked up, medicated, and put in a straight jacket. Instead I healed. Yes, I repeat. Instead, I healed. This book is a testimony to that. Instead of the crazy person I was about to be labelled and about to become, I came out the other side.

And why did I stay? As I stated in the introduction about the story of Ajahn Chah in his meditation practise where he couldn't go forward, he couldn't go back and he couldn't stand still – this is where I was at.

I couldn't leave the monastery as I had nowhere to go and was so self-destructive that I wouldn't have survived more than a few days. I couldn't kill myself for the reasons of what the Buddhists believed would happen to me. And I couldn't stand still because the hatred flowing over me in every moment would consume me some days. And so this is why I stayed. I had no choice. I had to stay – there was literally no other option. I wish looking back that there had been an easier way. Oh, you would not believe how much on earth I wished that it had been easier. I cry now just wishing it had been different. But on another level through this extreme suffering, through being in a hell realm really, I came out the other side. And I came out the other side with a little wisdom. When your back is against the wall and you have no other choice, in this place you do find a solution.

Gradually, very slowly, I started to heal. I did have the most amazing help you could imagine. Not only did I have the monks to call upon at any moment of the day, but I also started to work with one of the top Jungian analysts in the country, if not the world. She had been a contemporary of Jung and had been friends with Anelia Jaffe, Jung's personal assistant. She was in her 80s now and was a supporter of the monastery. I had tried other therapists locally but found that I was too cunning for them and even after months and months felt like I was getting nowhere. I remember bringing one therapist to tears with my story.

But Bani Shorter was very different. It was like I had someone to push against, to argue with, to prove how terrible a person I was. But she wouldn't have any of it. I had started to paint while in the monastery and she welcomed it. I was still painting in black and white when she suggested some colour – I have not looked back since then using paint as a way of dealing with emotions as they arose. Every week on Wednesday I would make a 7 hour round trip to work with her in Scotland. Our sessions were flexible. Sometimes they would last up to 4 hours. By her request I started to record my dreams, or should I say nightmares every night. It seemed like it was over a year that I would wake each night crying having had another nightmare. My unconscious knew that I was listening and started to pour out all my troubles, anxieties and pain in the form of these terrible nightmares. And each week I would send these dreams through to Bani. I worked very hard on my dreamwork spending sometimes an hour or 2 in the middle of the night writing my dreams down. Another monk started working with Bani at the same time, but he was reluctant to put the work in so stopped seeing her after a couple of months. It was painful work but I was starting to see light.

When I had arrived in the monastery the Abbot had taken me on a walk around the local lake. I remember the walk clearly and I remember exactly where we were when he asked me what my hobbies were. I reflected for a few moments and then said, rather embarrassed, drinking and watching football. I literally had no other hobbies. But as my time in the monastery grew so too did my hobbies. I was self-destructive and crazy at times but I started to feed myself as well. I started to paint, to do yoga, qigong, falun gong, draw, write – poetry and journals, I started to learn how to spot birds by sound and sight, I was walking, going to galleries on my trips to Scotland. There were signs of life. Little by little, step-by-step, breath-by-breath, baby step-by-baby step I started to heal.
But when you work non-stop and abuse yourself physically as I was doing something has to give. And something did give. Something definitely gave. One morning after being in the monastery about a year and a half I found I could hardly get out of bed. And my mind was a fuzz. I figured I had a bug and would get over it, but no, it stayed. I couldn't think straight any more Maybe it was my saviour as I no longer had the energy to beat myself as I had been doing. I was never diagnosed as having Chronic Fatigue or ME but having read books on the subject since I see this is what I had. From having as sharp a mind as one could have, remembering the tiniest of details (which worked totally against me remembering my childhood) suddenly I was not able to remember what I had done 2 hours ago, let alone yesterday.

But I plodded along step-by-step. It became a challenge getting to Scotland every week so Bani and I started to work by phone. And although over the years my energy levels increased a bit and my mind cleared somewhat, while in the monastery they never totally recovered. My emotions on the other hand definitely started to heal. The self-beatings became rarer and rarer and I learned to restrain myself and find new ways of dealing with my rage. It felt like having not cried for nearly 15 years, and spending the next 2 years crying nearly every day making up for the missed tears meant that I felt empty. After so many years of rage this was very pleasant indeed.

It took between 2 – 3 years to turn the corner. Looking back that is a long time. An awfully long time, especially in a monastery where time ticks along slowly. But somehow even though it was hellish at times I kept going.

And life would slowly start to change again.

Recap for Deepening Your Rest & Sleep

So what are the important points that we have covered in this chapter?

- **Set things up so you get a good night's sleep**. Sleeping well reduces your stress levels
- **Meditation before sleep** is a wonderful way of relaxing the mind and preparing you for sleep
- **Have a period of around an hour before going to sleep** where you start to slow down, read a gentle novel or meditate
- **Make your sleeping space a sacred space** where you only sleep, relax or be intimate. Put plants in your bedroom and make it a tidy and well-loved space
- **Get out of bed if you can't sleep** in the middle of the night and read a gentle novel or meditate. Don't watch TV or do work as this will not help you to go back to sleep
- **Have a lie-in a couple of times a week**
- **Use a black out sheet on your windows** to keep the light out to help you to sleep
- **Use earplugs or practise breathing techniques** if there is noise keeping you awake
- **Make sure you have a comfortable bed** as this will help you to sleep
- **Keep your bedroom at 16-18°C** during the night
- **Drink camomile tea** and keep off caffeine and chocolate before going to bed
- **Make sure you eat your evening meal several hours before bed** or this could keep you awake
- **Breathe deeply if you do wake in the night**

Chapter Nine – Questions

1. Name 3 ways which will help you to sleep better.

2. Name 1 thing you can do if you wake in the night.

3. What is good to drink before going to bed?

4. What are 4 things that will stimulate your mind before sleeping (all the answers are in the previous chapter)?

CHAPTER 10

Improving Your Relationships With Friends and Colleagues

Friends and colleagues are people who, second to your family, are those you spend the most time with. In some cases you spend more time with your work colleagues than you do with your family!

The modern trend does seem to be that we spend less time at home and more at work. We spend more time conversing with work colleagues than we do with our own wives or husbands.

So your relationships with your friends and colleagues are really important. If you are constantly with people who criticize and put you down your day is not going to be a pleasant one. Your self worth is not going to be very high.

So what can you do?

93. Choose Your Friends Wisely

Do you have friends in your life who wear you out and make you feel stressed every time you see them?

Do you have friends who make you feel alive, who fill you with wonder and excitement at the joy of living?

And which friends do you spend most of the time with? Do you spend your life sorting your friends' problems out rather than sorting out your own stress levels?

Ask yourself these questions:

a. Do you feel nurtured with certain friends and not so by others?
b. Do you feel good about yourself but then when you spend time with certain people you suddenly feel depressed or just plain miserable?
c. Which friends and colleagues do you feel nurtured around?

I came to a realisation a few years ago that I had a few friends who added very little to me and were always complaining. I felt tired and depressed after spending a few hours with them.

Now I didn't really do anything to stop the friendship. But that realisation in itself meant that I wasn't going to make much of an effort to keep in touch.

And what happened? Yes, they just fell away. I didn't contact them and they didn't contact me.

But a lot of times we keep friendships going out of duty. Duty to something or someone even if we can no longer remember what it is. It is like a routine but a healthy routine.

Now this doesn't mean that we have to end all unpleasant relationships but it does mean that we can put boundaries in place.

If someone is always complaining, you can say that you don't want to hear about their complaints all the time. The first time you do this, the reaction could be hostile: they are used to dumping their rubbish on you.

You could also ask them the question if they are talking about what they don't want, "So what do you want?" This will help them to focus on what they do want, focus on the positive and help to lift them.

Once you have laid down the boundary of what you are willing to accept or not, your friends will know where you stand.

There is a saying that says; sometimes by being kind to ourselves we upset others. I feel that if your intention is to be kind to yourself and in doing this others get offended, then for me, that's okay.

For example, a friend calls. They are upset again. But you are tired, you've worked a 7 day week, the kids are playing up and you need to rest. By being kind to both you and them you say, "Sorry I am going to bed. I will call you soon."

This is likely to upset your friend. But again that is okay. Your intention is to be kind to yourself primarily. That is our role in life, to look after ourselves first.

But that's selfish you say!

Not at all, if as in the example above, you did spend hours on the phone to your friend, you would not be giving good advice because you were so tired. You would be doing them a disservice – you might get angry at them or angry at yourself when you feel so worn out later on that evening.

The truth is that you would be doing them a service by looking after yourself. When you do call a few days later when you are refreshed and well again, the advice you give will reflect that.

You might struggle with this for a while but that is okay. See yourself as in the process of learning how to communicate positively with your friends and colleagues.

94. Find Several Good and Compassionate Friends to Spend Time With

If you don't have any people you could call good and compassionate people in your life, then I recommend that you find some. How? Join a group which you are passionate about, that might be sports, spirituality or tiddlywinks!

By having people in your life who not only understand you but are interested by you, you develop a wonderful support network. Not only does this make you feel part of a group and therefore not lonely but also develops your passions in life.

When you develop and take part in what you are passionate about you start to really enjoy life. And when you enjoy life? Your well-being flows.

And when things are not going as you would wish them, you then have people you can either spend time with to raise your mood or people to chat with. Sometimes not talking about a problem but focusing on fun and joy instead helps to shift how you are feeling.

95. Learn to Receive Others' Help

When it comes to friendships it is important to give and take. Remember taking is okay. Just as giving is okay, so is taking. And yet in the West when someone offers us help we are reluctant to receive it. Energy flows in, energy flows out – it is the nature of the universe – light becomes dark, day becomes night, yin becomes yang... When you stop the energy coming in, you stop the energy. It no longer flows.

By learning to receive others help in relationships and in friendships you keep this energy flowing. And on one level you are giving huge amounts to the other person. You are offering them a gift by receiving their love and generosity. Giving is a wonderful blessing and by you receiving it graciously you allow the other person to feel the wondrous feeling of giving.

Be aware that if you are asking for people's help on one level but then don't receive it when they offer, this is stopping the flow of good things into your life – relationships, money, success, love…

So start to ask for help when you need it and then receive it. Start receiving yourself. Start to see that it is okay to receive. Being human is a balance of giving and receiving. You cannot give all the time without burning yourself out.

Give and receive. Swallow that pride and ask for help when it is needed. And then receive the good that is always flowing your way.

96. Having a Break From Friends

Sometimes we can be afraid of being on our own so we fill our time so that we are always with others.

But in a lot of cases you need to have down time, time alone to collect your thoughts and come back to centre. By doing this you reduce your stress levels dramatically and fill yourself with well-being.

Sure there is a time for socialising but there is also a time for resting. Balance is so key in well-being. This comes back to the previous point on giving and receiving. Sometimes the body needs to be on the receiving end of some TLC administered by you.

I find that sometimes I lose a sense of who I am and where I am going if I spend too much time with friends or lovers. I need, as part of being who I am, to have time alone.

This time alone can nourish you, give you sustenance for the rainy days ahead, and give you direction again so that you know that all is well and that you are on the right path. Without this you can become stressed because you might start to lose direction. You might start to lose what you are truly passionate about, and start living your life according to others values rather than your own. So find some time for yourself, on your own, doing something you love and fill yourself up.

97. Getting Support From Friends

Friends are a truly important part of your inner toolbox to coping with stress. When things get difficult then you can call a friend or have a chat. Sharing with a wise and loving being can really help to lift your spirits and help you get perspective.

I personally learned this in the Buddhist monastery I lived in. In the beginning I was too stubborn to ask for help as you know. I was a martyr. I was attached to my pain as it was my identity. I felt that it made me who I was.

The abbot made me an offer to me after I'd been in the monastery a while. He said that if I needed to speak to him then just come and find him and if he was available he would help.

But to start off with I would prefer to cry and crucify myself rather than disturb him. I was stuck in many patterns of pain and destruction and didn't understand what an amazing offer that was.

But after a little time, I got the hint. I let go (a small bit) of the poor me syndrome, the needy wounded child and went to him.

And of course he helped me beyond belief. I am here talking to you about it now...

So don't be frightened of asking friends for help when you need it. Obviously it is important that you don't become the person who dumps all their rubbish on others, but do ask for help if needed.

Another of the monks also really helped me while I was going through my challenging times. He was always there for me when I needed help; such a magnificent soul. And why did he help me so much? Because he too had had challenging times in his life as well and therefore knew how I felt; compassion, he had compassion.

And this is why I am here. I feel that my experiences have great value in them for others. I know that my experiences can be of service to others so that they can move towards well-being without the challenges that I went through. So find friends, use the resources at hand, and try not to be too stubborn!

98. What to Do With Negative Work Colleagues

We have all worked with them and we have all despaired at times. But to have negative work colleagues who create a lot of stress in your life does not have to be as bad as it is.

There is a thing called the law of attraction. And this law states **like attracts like**.

This is to say that like minded people will congregate together. The negative sit with the negative, the positive people with the positive.

The first step if you have lots of negative work colleagues around you is to ask: what am I doing to attract this? Yes, this law starts with you. What are you giving off to attract these negative people.

Think about it. If you have a group of people who are complaining all the time and this is what they love doing, they will only attract others to their group who like to complain.

Someone who is positive will just sit in silence or will challenge them. And it will not be long before the positive person will get up and leave or the negative people will not want to spend time with the positive person.

Are you always complaining? Maybe not to others but in your own head? If you are complaining in your own head how do you think your facial expressions are? Do you think they are happy and radiant? Or do you think you will have a permanent scowl on your face?

So this is in essence how the law of attraction applies here: people will be negative around people they feel comfortable doing so. Do you think people go up to the Dalai Lama and start complaining? Or do you think that they tell him what a wonderful being he is? Or do they just not know what to say?

What are you giving off? Realize that it is your responsibility to change your internal dialogue. If you don't you will keep attracting more negative and stressful situations into your life.

Do you want your life to be stressful or peaceful? You choose...

Isn't that empowering?

99. Seeing What You Do Want With Colleagues

It can be very easy to blame others for your stress or your anxiety. In some cases this might make you feel better but this is usually just a temporary fix.

What is the solution?

I personally think that if you allow and encourage your work colleagues to gossip about others and you indulge in it, then you can't blame them. You have responsibility here. You are no longer the child who has to listen and not interrupt.

If you are with people who are gossiping around you, don't get drawn in. Keep seeing these people in all their shininess (their brilliance) and in this case, see them as saying lovely things about other people. The more you do this the less you will find yourself around the people who are gossiping anyway.

When you feel anger or annoyance at people who are gossiping and being derogatory about other people take responsibility for what you are feeling. Remember these are your feelings. If you share this feeling with the people who are gossiping then you might well get that same anger or frustration coming back to you.

Your responsibility is you. You take care of what you are feeling and then start to see your colleagues, friends, lovers in all their positive aspects. Stop giving the focus to their negative traits (and we all have these) and start to focus on the benevolent qualities that your friends, colleagues and lovers do have. And when you focus on this, what happens, you get more and more of what you do want coming towards you.

100. Smile At Your Colleagues

This is one practice that I did to all my colleague when I was working for corporate America. I was working in a big office and there were around 100 people sat at desks in this open plan office.

Whenever I would walk past people or be stood at the coffee machine I would smile or say hello.

This does two things. Firstly it raises your own energy and level of happiness. Try smiling now. How does it feel? Good? I am sure it does.

Secondly, it raises the energy of your colleague – they too feel good about themselves. They might not smile to start off with – you might have caught them off guard, lost in their own thoughts, but smile anyhow. The next time you see this colleague they will remember you and smile back when you smile.

And continue smiling at people even if you don't get a response – eventually they will smile every one does in the end.

But remember to give from your heart. This means don't expect anything in return. Give as you would give an unconditional gift – completely without expectation of return. If you are expecting a smile back from someone else and you don't get it, you'll just end up getting upset and this is not the point of the exercise – stress relief remember!

101. Raising The Vibration Of A Conversation

I have worked with certain groups as a support worker and in many offices. Certain people have a tendency to be very critical when they are talking. This is to say that all they do is complain and criticize others.

Now there is no blame here – this is just their way. But it doesn't mean that you have to sit and listen to it.

One way of deflecting negativity is to start to allow your eyes to wander when the person starts going there. Look as if you have lost interest. Another way is to directly say, "I prefer not to talk about this, please."

Another way to change the conversation is through praise. We have this modern way that we have to put others down all the time – in a jokey manner of course. When challenged people say, oh I am only joking. Nasty comments and put downs are nasty comments and put downs even if they are said as a joke.

On the other hand people thrive off praise. When you see something worthy of praise say it. Tell them how good they look, how it is good to see them.

When working as a support worker I used to get made cups of hot water – and they were always really tasty. So I would compliment the lady who made them – I really praised her. And the result was after a few months she came up to me and said that she had started to drink hot water too. She said that she thought it must be good for her as I seemed to be enjoying it so much. Here was a lady who I had found quite negative and critical of others in the beginning but through praise and kindness softened and became receptive to new ideas.

So we do affect those around us in both a positive and negative way. If you are always positive this rubs off on others and this makes them feel good. They see another way of being - they might not change, but at least they see there is another way.

And if you criticize and put others down this too rubs off on others – you attract more people who are negative and situations for you to complain about.

Another way of changing the tone of a conversation is to follow what was outlined in the previous point – that of seeing the other person in all their shining – see them praising others. The law of attraction says that we wouldn't attract negative, critical people if there wasn't some aspect of it within us. So when someone negative is complaining see it is an opportunity to clear this pattern within you and see this person and as praising others and saying wonderful things. You will feel great and you will then start to attract people who praise and say wonderful things.

102. Remember That Nobody Is Perfect

Often when we are looking for friends or relationships for that matter, we are sometimes looking for the perfect person. They have to be like this, they have to be able to do this, or they have to own this.

I think discernment is great – it is important to set your lower limits when looking for friends and partners – that which you are not prepared to go below e.g. someone who swears all the time, someone who gets into fights or is abusive.

But I also think that sometimes people can be too discerning and therefore nobody is good enough for them.

Although you might not be putting your friends down to their faces maybe you put them down in your own mind, "Oh, they're no good at this," "My friends are so uncouth!"

But what you will be doing is attracting to you people who do not have high self-esteem. You will attract to you people who are okay with being criticized, because internally you will be criticizing them.

What can you do?

Learn to start to see the good qualities in your friends. Have a bottom line of what you are not prepared to go below but from then on really focus on what is good in others. Praise them; see what good qualities they have – maybe it's being so patient around you even when you are being stressed and anxious.

And by focusing on their good qualities you start to feed them. Not only do your friends feel good and nourished around you but they also like being around you. And this rubs off on you – it becomes great fun being around your friends – you feel more relaxed.

So when thinking of your friends do you always focus on what is bad in them rather than what is wonderful? Do you always want them to be other than they are? When you stop trying to change others, they relax. You've stopped criticizing them, putting them down; you start to receive them as they are.

So don't be hard on others and especially don't be hard on yourself. Be kind, be kind.

It was mid 2005 and I was still living in the monastery. I went away for a break to visit friends and family - after period of a few years where I had blocked contact with my mother and sister, I reconnected. When I came back from the trip away the Abbot asked me whether I wanted to continue at the monastery. Each year we had spoken about whether we were both happy with my continuing as a Novice. He asked to know within a specific time.

I went away and reflected. I didn't know. I was feeling better than I had been in years and felt I could go back out into the outside world again. Did I want to? Life was still a challenge in the monastery as my energy levels had never recovered fully so I had to be careful of what I did. What should I do? I still didn't know. I made a choice and knew that whatever the choice may be it was the correct one. So I decided to leave. I arrived with 2 bags and was going to stay 10 days. I ended up staying over 1000 days! What a roller-coaster ride that was!

I had done no paid work for 3 and a half years so all my savings had been spent. I had a few shares left and sold them to give me a few thousand pounds as a buffer while I found my feet. I set off for the sun for a month while also visiting Mother Meera, a spiritual teacher based in Germany.

I have many stories and many tales not yet told but just to say that being in the outside world was not as bad any more; I could cope. And I was doing pretty well. I was painting a lot, my meditation practise deepened like I had never known and I felt good in myself.

My sister gave me a sum of money from an inheritance and for a year I painted, I wrote, I started to work with another Jungian therapist in Brighton and my energy levels started to increase.

I ran out of funds after a year and as I wanted to continue working with my Jungian analyst I applied for some jobs in the corporate world. It was not what I wanted and was hugely resistant but with the support of my analyst I took the plunge and got offered a job working as the UK Delivery Query Coordinator for a huge international toilet paper company.

It was a challenge, to be sure, especially that first week sat in an office with 100 other people. But with each challenge I rose to it. Instead of folding, returning to drink, drugs or sex I used what I had learned in the monastery – I kept my meditation practise going, kept off the drink, kept learning and growing.

And my colleagues wanted to know more about my experiences. And within a short space of time I started teaching stress management and well-being to my colleagues. It felt great. I started recording videos, talks, created a website, started writing regularly and ran classes.

From being where I was in the gutter to being able to share what I learned felt an honour. After a year and a half of working in the corporate world I left so that I could start studying shamanism in the north of England. I worked looking after children, recorded children's meditation CDs and studied. I spent 5 years studying shamanism, and kept learning other paradigms, from qualifying as a hypnotherapist, to NLP, to EFT, from law of attraction to qigong, from raw food to becoming a Reiki Master, from meditation practises to sacred geometry. And then I met my most amazing teacher yet, Michelle Dawn Silcox, who later became my wife (but that is a whole other story in and of itself).

This book and these tools, as you now know are from my personal experience. I teach them to you because they have worked for me in the most extreme of circumstances. And if I can do it, you can do it too. You can enter into the stream of well-being that is your birthright because you are an amazing, brilliant, being of light. I know from my own extreme conditioning that we are led to believe and taught to think otherwise – that we are anything but worthy of love, joy and peace. But through using and applying these tools in this book you can start to enter into a space where you realize that you are worthy, you are worthy of joy and love.

It is yours.

You are amazing.

Thank you for reading this book, for joining me on my journey. There have been many tears writing this book but it has been an honour.

Recap on Improving Your Relatonships With Friends and Colleagues

We have covered the following points about how to improve your relationships with friends and colleagues:

- **Choose your friends wisely** – see that certain friends feed you and certain don't and that you have a choice with whom you spend your time
- **Find several good and compassionate friends** to spend time with
- **Learn to receive others help**, if you are asking for help but not listening to people's advice, people will stop advising you.
- If you are always with friends, **having a break** from them can be really nourishing for yourself and will help you to see their wonderful qualities.
- **Getting support from friends** when you are feeling stressed or anxious or depressed is a really important tool for pulling yourself through – use it.
- If you have negative work colleagues **don't indulge in their gossip** – talk about positive things and see them in their shining.
- **Putting boundaries down with colleagues** is really important if you want to stop them criticizing or gossiping to you. Only if you tell them will they know to stop. But do it from a place of kindness.
- **Smile at your colleagues** when walking around the office.
- You can raise the vibration of a conversation by **praising others** and by not being drawn into negative conversations.
- **Remember that nobody is perfect** – give your friends and colleagues a break and learn to see the good in everyone.

Chapter Ten – Questions

1. Make a list of friends who really feed you? Who lifts your spirits when you talk to them?

2. What are the qualities that you look for in a friend?

3. Look at the people around you in your life. What are you really grateful for in them?

4. What are the ways you can start to raise the vibration in the place you work?

CHAPTER 11

Summary Questions

You have now completed How To Survive and Thrive in Challenging Times. Well done. I mean it, well done. It takes initiative and determination to first of all do something about stress and challenges and move into well-being.

And by reading through and doing something about your challenges, well, this is a totally different level of things. You will change and you are changing your life by doing this.

The following questions will help you to see how much you have learned and what areas you need to cover again. So what have you learned?

Chapter One: Exercise

What 3 ways can you relieve stress with exercise?

1.

2.

3.

Chapter Two: Finances, Wealth & Money

What 3 things have you learned about wealth and how will you implement them?

1.

2.

3.

Chapter Three: Spirituality

What 3 techniques have you learned in this chapter which will affect the way you approach life and others?

1.

2.

3.

Chapter Four: Work

Name 3 techniques for reducing your work stress

1.

2.

3.

Chapter Five: Health & Diet

What are 3 foods which are super health foods and will reduce your stress levels?

1.

2.

3.

Chapter Six: Holidays

Name 3 tips for reducing your holiday stress.

1.

2.

3.

Chapter Seven: Relationships With Others

What 3 ways can you improve your personal relationships?

1.

2.

3.

Chapter Eight: Home

How do you reduce the stress created in your own home. What 3 things can you do to reduce this stress?

1.

2.

3.

Chapter Nine: Sleep & Rest

What 3 ways can you improve your sleep?

1.

2.

3.

Chapter Ten: Friends & Colleagues

In what 3 ways can you reduce the stress you feel around friends and colleagues?

1.

2.

3.

EPILOGUE

Yesterday I was visiting with one of the monks I had lived with in the monastery. I was telling him some of the stories I had just put in this book. He looked at me and said that his experience had been that people don't really change. And yet listening to things I had got up to – drink, drugs, aggression and how I was now he said that he saw people can change.

And yes people can change. I have changed. You can change. Wherever you feel you are, you can change. It is possible. And with the help of these tools you will find the strength within, that is already within you, to change.

So where am I now? On an emotional level I feel in a better place than I have ever felt in my life. My heart has opened although there are days when the doors close. I have my work to do. I am now married to an amazing woman who has been instrumental in helping me to open my heart. From literally feeling very little emotionally pre-monastery to now being able to cry when something upsets me, to laughing when something over-joys me is a magnificent change in my life.

I still have my stuff, my baggage, my patterns, but they are not as pronounced as before. I no longer punch holes in the wall or physically beat myself. I get angry or upset from time to time, but I now see it as a gift, as energy, rather than something terrible. I now use this energy to transform myself. It sometimes takes me a little time but I now have the tools available to me to change.

I still make my mistakes from time to time, and over the years since leaving the monastery I have made plenty. Yet these mistakes, these so called failures have been my greatest gifts. They have been instrumental in allowing me to see what I do want in life. And they have allowed me to grow into a more balanced human being.

And yet there have also been many successes over the years. I have grown, I have developed as a man, as a husband, as a friend, to others and to myself. It has now been nearly 12 years since I last had an alcoholic drink or smoked any marijuana. That is a big success for me even if I forget this from time to time. I have manifested around me a great abundance of health, - physical, emotional, spiritual, mental and sexual wellness.

But I have realized over the past few months that it is now time for my story to be told so that it can be of service to others. I have been hiding away from others, mainly out of fear of what people would think of me and my story. I have been frightened that my family would reject me again for speaking my truth. But that is my stuff. I am here to be of service and I feel that I have been doing everything rather than share the information in this book. Over the last few years I have been doing everything but getting this book published. It is time now. And as it is in your hands, the time is right, and the time has come.

So my final words to you are that life can be a challenge and for most people it is a challenge on one level or other. But through this challenge as I have shown in this book with these tools and stories you can grow and develop into a truly magnificent, amazing, and shiny being. You can become the all that you are already. It is within you. Every resource is within you now, in this moment, now. And with these tools and words you move closer to your magnificence. Sometimes all it takes is a breath, in and then out.

Life is not meant to be as challenging as we make it out to be. Life is meant to be good, to be juicy, to be joyful. And in this moment you can choose joy, love, connection, bliss. They are all yours.

So go out into this world – shine your light – be the all that you are. You are so worth it.

I love you,
May you be well,

Piers Cross

MORE INFORMATION

For more information about working with me on a 1-1 basis then please get in touch. I specialise in helping people with anxiety, boarding school issues and overcoming trauma. Please visit https://www.piers-cross.com/coaching

For information about retreats and workshops that I run please visit the website.

https://www.piers-cross.com

HOW TO Survive
& Thrive
In Challenging Times

To follow me on social media:

Facebook	https://www.facebook.com/pierscrosspublic
Linked in	https://www.linkedin.com/in/piers-cross/
YouTube	https://www.youtube.com/user/pierscross

BIBLIOGRAPHY

Guide to Natural Healing – Geddes and Grosset
The Secret – Rhonda Burns
Food for the Heart – Ajahn Chah
The Dhammapada – Ajahn Munindo
The Science of Getting Rich – Wallace Wattles
How to make one Hell of a Profit and still get to Heaven – Dr John Demartini
The Science of Being Great – Wallace Wattles
The Greatest Money Making Secret – Joe Vitale
The Magic of Thinking Big – David J Swartz
The Flower of Life Vol 1 – Drunvalo Melchizedek
The Flower of Life Vol 2 – Drunvalo Melchizedek
Living in the Heart – Drunvalo Melchizedek
Being Dharma: The Essence of the Buddha's Teachings by Ajahn Chah
Bodinyana – Ajahn Chah
No Ajahn Chah – Ajahn Chah
The Path to Peace – Ajahn Chah
The Gift Of Well-Being – Ajahn Munindo
Unexpected Freedom – Ajahn Munindo
The Way It Is – Ajahn Sumedho
Teachings of a Buddhist Monk – Ajahn Sumedho
Mindfulness, the path to the deathless: The meditation teaching of Venerable Ajahn Sumedho – Ajahn Sumedho
The Four Noble Truths - Ajahn Sumedho
Now is The Knowing – Ajahn Sumedho
Cittaviveka – Ajahn Sumedho
Freeing the Heart - Dhamma teaching from the Nuns' Community
The Alchemist – Paulo Coelho
Conversations with God – Neale Donald Walsch
The Celestine Prophecy – James Redfield
You Can Heal Your Life – Louise Hay

ACKNOWLEDGEMENTS

This book would not have happened without the support of the monks, and the lay supporters of the monastery. Thank you so much from the bottom of my heart.

To Michelle Dawn Silcox, my wife and the most amazing woman I have ever met. Your wisdom flows through this book. I have learned so many things from you and so much of the teachings in this book have come from you. Thank you beautiful, amazing woman.

To my step-son Ryan. I have learned so much from you. You are a really wise young man and see you as a real gift to this world.

To William Verling, for supporting me as a friend for so many years and giving me a bed when I was homeless.

To Bani Shorter and Paul Goldreich, the Jungian analysts who helped to change my inner world.

To my family, for your support and love.

To Christy Lacroix for her amazing work with the book formatting and book cover. Thank you so much for your generosity and attention to detail. I so appreciate it.

To all my friends who have supported me on my journey and with reading the manuscript and giving me feedback.

To all the teachers I have studied with over the years helping me to grow.

To the Scouts I look after for helping me to become a better person.

And thank you to all my clients and students for helping me to grow as a coach and therapist and for trusting me.

Printed in Great Britain
by Amazon

50982116R10159